IT STARTS WITH YOU

How to Raise Happy, Successful Children
By Becoming the Best Role Model
You Can Possibly Be

— A Guidebook for Parents —

IT STARTS WITH YOU

How to Raise Happy, Successful Children
By Becoming the Best Role Model
You Can Possibly Be

— A Guidebook for Parents —

Dr. Suzanne Gelb, PhD, JD

FIRST EDITION

———————

All rights reserved. This book or any portion thereof may not be reproduced or used in any manner whatsoever without the express written permission of the publisher except for the use of brief quotations in a book review.

Copyright © 2019 Suzanne J. Gelb, Ph.D., J.D.

Manufactured in the United States of America.

ISBN-13: 978-0692647394
ISBN-10: 0692647392

www.DrSuzanneGelb.com

OTHER BOOKS BY THE AUTHOR

―――――――

How to Get Your Kids to Cooperate and Help Them Become the Best Grown-Ups They Can Be. (A Life Guide.)

Helping Your Teen Make Healthy Choices About Dating and Sex.

How to Get Ready to Be a Parent and Be the Best Mom or Dad You Can Possibly Be. (A Life Guide.)

How to Forgive the One Who Hurt You Most. (A Life Guide.)

How to Deal With People Who Drive You Absolutely Nuts.

Aging With Grace, Strength and Self-Love. (A Life Guide.)

How to Navigate Being Single and Savor Your Dating Adventure.

The Love Tune-Up: How to Amp Up the Love That's Naturally Inside You to Enjoy Happy, Healthy Relationships.

How to Rekindle That Spark and Create the Relationship and Sex Life That You Want. (A Life Guide.)

How to Find Work That You Love When You're Stuck in a Job That You Hate. (A Life Guide.)

How to Reach Your Ideal Weight Through Kindness, Not Craziness. (A Life Guide.)

Welcome Home: Release Addictions and Return to Love.

How to Care for Yourself When You're a Caregiver for Somebody Else. (A Life Guide.)

DEDICATION

This book is dedicated to parents everywhere.

As a parent, you have one of the most important jobs on the planet and unlike other "jobs," you never get a "day off" from this job. Even when you're not physically in the same room as your child, you are still their parent, their guardian, their primary influencer, their role model. You are a parent forever. That's no small responsibility!

This book is for you... to support you, encourage you, provide some useful, applicable ideas, and hopefully, make your job a little simpler.

Thank you for doing all that you do. You matter.

This book is also dedicated to children everywhere.

To every child: you are a blessing, you are loved, and you were born for a reason.

You matter, too.

ACKNOWLEDGEMENTS

This book was a labor of love.

Lots of people labored (very lovingly) and poured a lot of time, energy and care into every single page to produce this book for you.

I'd like to thank...

- Woz Flint for her eagle-eyed proofreading.
- Alexandra Franzen for her structural ideas and writing assistance.
- Dr. Susan Mathison for contributing a lovely foreword.
- My mentor and dearest friend, JW, for years of guidance and support. (JW, I still feel your beautiful presence, even though you are no longer living here on this earth.)
- The many men, women, and families who sought me out for psychotherapy, life coaching, and parenting counseling recently and over the past several decades. To all the people who have stepped into my office for a session, or who have spoken to me on the phone, or who have sent in an email with a burning question about children, parenting, or how to resolve a tricky issue at home... every single moment has influenced my work and ultimately, has led to me creating this book.

Thank you, all of you, deeply and fully.
This book wouldn't be here without your love.

CONTENTS

Foreword by Susan Mathison, MD — xxiii

Disclaimer — xxvii

Introduction — 1

HOW THIS BOOK IS ORGANIZED AND WHAT TO READ FIRST — 5

THE BASICS — 8

CHAPTER ONE

"My child won't cooperate!" — 11

What is "positive discipline"? — 12
"Why is it so hard to implement 'the rules' sometimes?" — 14
Rules and consequences: what's age-appropriate? — 15
"How much 'reminding' should I do?" — 24
"What about giving rewards for good behavior?" — 26
Closing words: Christie's happy ending. — 27

CHAPTER TWO

"My child is so manipulative! He's always playing one parent against the other." — 29

"What if my spouse or co-parent and I CANNOT agree?" — 32
Closing words: Resolution and unity, at last. — 33

CHAPTER THREE

"My child is an underachiever. Why won't he reach his potential?"   36

What causes a child to develop low self-esteem?   37
Finding solutions.   39
Closing words: Aiming for "excellence" not "perfection."   40

CHAPTER FOUR

"My child is so stressed all the time. Why is she such a perfectionist?"   41

What causes "overachieving"?   41
"But isn't being 'the best' a good thing?"   43
Closing words: Abby's new chapter.   44

CHAPTER FIVE

"My child makes such bad decisions! Terrible time management. Procrastination. Why can't she get it together?"   46

Why do children get disorganized and procrastinate?   47
"But c'mon, she's just a kid!"   48
A solution for time-management and organizational issues   50
Closing words: Order, at last!   51

CHAPTER SIX

"My child has terrible manners! She's so rude and inconsiderate."   53

Why do "good children" become "rude little monsters"?   54
Closing words: Sophia's turnaround.   58

CHAPTER SEVEN

"My child is shy and has a hard time making friends."   60

Why are some children so shy?   60
Self-reflection.   61
Finding solutions.   62
Closing words: Coming out of her shell.   63

CHAPTER EIGHT

"My child is overweight."   64

Model healthy "emotional management."   66
STOP the crash dieting.   67
Closing words: Making progress, together.   68

CHAPTER NINE

"My child is dating and might be having sex. I'm so worried."   70

Why does this situation happen?   71
Supervision, rules, and consequences.   74
Closing words: It's never too late to influence your teen.   77

CHAPTER TEN

"My child is tech-addicted! I can't get him to unplug from his phone."   78

What's my relationship with technology?   79
Finding solutions.   80
Parental role modeling is huge.   81
Closing words: Respect tech, strive for balance.   81

CHAPTER ELEVEN

"My child is being bullied and teased at school."   83

Finding solutions.   84
Get informed.   87
Closing words: From "victim" to "problem solver."   88

CHAPTER TWELVE

"My child is having trouble adjusting to a new home / school situation."   89

Why do children have difficulty adapting and adjusting?   89
Finding solutions.   91
Closing words: New home, same routines, happier children.   94

CHAPTER THIRTEEN

"My child 'hates' me. I'm heartbroken."   96

Why do kids lash out and say hurtful things like, "I hate you!"?   97
Finding solutions.   97
Closing words: Clear rules, no guilt.   100

CHAPTER FOURTEEN

"My child won't talk to me."   103

Why do children "clam up" and refuse to talk?   103
"Is it 'normal' for teenagers to sulk or be silent and moody?"   105
Finding solutions.   108
Closing words: Interruption-free communication, happier children!   109

CHAPTER FIFTEEN

"We are going through a divorce. My child is so upset."   111

Guidelines for effective parenting during a divorce.   112
Closing words: De-stressing = better parenting.   117

CHAPTER SIXTEEN

"I keep losing my temper with my child. I don't know how to stop!"   119

Self-reflection   120
It's all possible. It starts with you!   121
Closing words: Not "that kind of mom" anymore!   124

CHAPTER SEVENTEEN

"I want to parent my child a certain way, but my child's other parent is not on the same page as me."   125

The fifteen second rule.   127
Finding solutions.   129
Closing words: Forgive and march on.   131

CHAPTER EIGHTEEN

"My child's grandparent / stepparent / babysitter is spoiling her! She's acting out because I'm not as 'nice' as the 'other' grown ups."   132

Why do "childcare conflicts" arise?   133
Self-reflection.   134
Closing words: Clear policies, more harmony.   139

CHAPTER NINETEEN

"I have one child who is highly successful and gets praise all of the time. I'm worried that my other child feels less loved."   141

Why do parents develop "favoritism" for one child over another?   142
Treating all of your children with love, attention, and affection, in equal amounts.   146
Closing words: A surprising phone call, a breakthrough, and... progress.   147

CHAPTER TWENTY

"I am struggling with something big and difficult right now (addiction, alcoholism, etc.) Honestly: I'm not OK. Can I still be an effective parent for my child?"   149

Can you be a "good parent" even if you're battling a big problem like an addiction?   150
Closing words: Recovery is possible. Progress is possible. Anything is possible.   154

Closing Words   157
Worksheets and Tools   158
Resources   170
About the Author   172
Praise for... *It Starts With You*   173

FOREWORD

There are three things I've always wanted:

To become a doctor, to become an entrepreneur, and to become a mom.

The good news is: All three of my dreams have come true.

I am a triple-board certified physician, the director of my own medical center, and the proud mama to Grant Mathison Johnson, a beautiful, inquisitive, rocket ship and weather-loving bundle of boyish joy.

The bad (well not "bad," but let's say, "honest") news is:

None of it has been "easy." Not in the past. Not in the present.

This is probably not a huge surprise. After all, nobody signs up for medical school and then hears, "Oh, good for you! Just sit back and relax. It's going to be a easy ride..." And nobody decides to become a parent and then hears, "Wonderful! Get ready for lots of deep sleep and calm, breezy times ahead..."

The path that I've chosen — the multiple roles that I've chosen to play in this lifetime — are undeniably demanding ones. I know this. I've known it all along. I knew that I was signing up for "big work." I knew, also, that it would all be worth it. And it is. And yet... even though it's all "worth it," it can still be very tough.

Like many working parents, every single day in our household feels like an intricate juggling act of logistics, priorities, and emotions. Like many moms, I've felt that all-too familiar twinge of guilt at leaving my kid with his nanny because "Mommy needs to work." Like many moms, I've watched, feeling helpless and frustrated, as Grant throws a tantrum — in public — at a restaurant or shop. I've struggled to gain Grant's cooperation (and convince him that broccoli is super exciting!) when he refuses to eat a nutritious meal. I've flopped into bed, exhausted after a long day at the clinic, feeling guilty because Grant wants a bedtime story and mommy is just so tired. I still try to read and occasionally doze off mid-sentence.

And like most (probably "all") parents, I've had bleak moments where I've wondered, "Am I doing this wrong?" or "Why won't he just listen?" or "Is there something I am missing — something my son needs, something that I could give him, to give him every possible chance at a happy, successful adult life?

These are the real-life, honest challenges of raising a child. These are the big questions that keep parents up at night — whether you have a job, run a business, or whether parenting is your full-time occupation. We all wonder about these things. We all struggle. Parenting is beautiful, it's a blessing, and also, it can feel challenging and messy.

That is why — when my colleague Dr. Suzanne Gelb told me, "I am writing a book with tools for parents on how to raise happy, well-adjusted kids" — I was thrilled.

Dr. Gelb has been working in the field of psychology, life coaching, and emotional health for close to 29 years. To top it off, she has also practiced law — focusing on family law. Through the decades, she has spent thousands of hours coaching and counseling men, women, couples, parents, and children, helping them to resolve all kinds of challenges, big and small. If there was ever a woman who could provide sage, seasoned advice on the topic of "parenting," she's it.

What I love most about Dr. Gelb's philosophy — and this book — is that she fundamentally believes that you, as a parent, are whole, are enough, that you already have the answers you need within you, and that if you focus on taking good care of yourself — eating well, sleeping well, managing your stress levels, being kind to yourself and others — then your child will see you, admire you, respect you, and instinctively follow in your footsteps.

By helping yourself, you help your child. By tending to your own needs, you set an example for your child. By taking steps to shine brighter in our world, you light the way for your child. As Dr. Gelb sums it up: *"It starts with you."*

This common-sense, "be a role model" approach to parenting is so refreshing. Deep down, every parent "knows," intuitively, that role-modeling is the key to effective parenting. We just get so frazzled and tired and overwhelmed by the complications of everyday life that sometimes, we forget.

This book — *It Starts With You* — feels like a beautiful reminder to slow down, stop worrying, and get back to basics. Back to thoughtful role modeling. Back to love.

Unconditional love for yourself. Unconditional love for your kids. Sensible rules and policies (for both of you) that allow you to thrive. And then, more love. Whether you're a parent or a child, you can never have too much love.

From one busy, imperfect, fiercely loving parent to another... remember that, no matter how challenging things get or how "bad" things have gotten at home, it is never too late to learn something new, to try something different, to tweak your routines, to change the household rules, to firmly enforce the rules that you've set (maybe for the first time, ever...) and to become an even stronger role model for your child. Dr. Gelb repeatedly enforces this idea — *"It is never, ever too late"* — throughout this book. It's a comforting, empowering idea — and it's true.

A better future for your child starts right here, in the pages of this book.

It starts with you.

Susan Mathison, M.D.

DISCLAIMER

This book is a resource to support you in gaining a greater understanding of how to...

- Become an effective role model for your children,
- Resolve frustrating conflicts and issues at home, and
- Raise happy, successful children who have every possible chance to grow up and become happy, successful adults.

This book contains educational exercises and tips drawn from my career in the field of emotional wellness with over 20 years of experience. This book is for informational purposes only, and is not intended to diagnose or treat any illness, nor is it a substitute for professional or psychological advice, diagnosis, or treatment. Always consult a qualified health care professional before engaging in any new, self-help resource (such as this one) and with questions you may have about your health and wellbeing.

Any case material indirectly alluded to in this book or in articles [see Resources section] does not constitute guarantees of similar outcomes for the reader. No results can be promised, since everyone's personal development path is unique.

Links inside this book to external websites are for informational purposes only. Linking does not imply endorsement of or affiliation with that site, its content, or any product or service it may offer.

All link URLs in this book are current at the time of printing. Link URLs may fail at some point if the page has been deleted or moved. The author assumes no responsibility or liability for broken links.

This concludes the disclaimer portion of this book.

INTRODUCTION

He walks into my office with a tortured look on his face.

This is a father who has clearly reached his wit's end. He doesn't want to be here in my office. He's here because he doesn't know what else to do.

Slumping into the chair in my office, he seems on the verge of tears.

"My son won't cooperate," he says. "Won't listen to anything I say. I think he actually hates me. I don't know how to make things better."

I nod. It's heartbreaking, but this father's pain is a particular kind of pain that I've seen hundreds of times before.

"So, what are you hoping to achieve in working with me?" I ask.

A pause.

"I just want my kid to be happy. To grow up and be a good person. Have a good life.

I want our home to feel peaceful again, not like a war zone. I just want all of us — me, my wife, my son — I want all of us to be happy."

I nod again.

"So let's talk about you," I begin.

"I thought we were going to talk about my son." he counters.

"We are," I confirm. "But we need to start by talking about you."

That's the reality about being a parent.

Raising a happy, successful child starts with you.

It always starts with you.

What do I mean when I say, "it starts with you"?

This isn't about pointing fingers or assigning blame.

It's simply about an actual fact.

As a parent, you are the single most influential factor in your child's life.

You are your child's primary role model.

Children, especially very young children under the age of six, absorb the world around them like a sponge. They look to you for cues on how to behave.

When you are stressed and don't know how to manage your stress in a healthy, productive way, that influences your child.

When you have emotional baggage from the past, and you carry that baggage around like a heavy, burdensome backpack, it influences your child.

When you make promises to yourself and others — "This year, I am really going to start taking better care of my body!" — and then you break those promises, that influences your child.

Everything you do and say influences your child, positively or negatively.

That's what I mean when I say: "it starts with you."

Already you might be thinking, "Well, great, except… my child doesn't listen to me or follow my instructions. How am I supposed to wield influence if my child doesn't take me seriously?"

To that, I would say:

If you want your child to listen to you, embrace your guidance, and follow your rules, you need to first earn your child's trust and respect. You need to become the kind of hero and role model that your child can rely on, count on, and admire.

What I have found, through academic research as well as real-world coaching and thousands of hours conversing with parents over the past 29 years, is this:

If you can earn your child's trust, then they are likely to follow your guidance.

OK, so now you might be thinking, "Well, sure. Makes sense. But what if my spouse / partner / ex-partner isn't on the same page as me? What if I become a terrific role model and earn my child's trust and respect, but my 'co-parent' doesn't? Is my child doomed?"

To that, I would respond:

It's always ideal when all of the influential adults in your child's life (parents, co-parents, spouses of co-parents, teachers, coaches, grandparents, babysitters, etc.) are on the same page, when it comes to parenting — presenting a consistent, united front. This gives your child a sense of security, knowing that they are being guided by dependable, committed adults who are working together in harmony.

However, even when that is not the case (which is quite often, sadly), I believe it is still possible for children to develop in a healthy way, even if there is only one dependable parent present.

That parent might need to be <u>you</u>.

So, here's my question for you:

Are you ready to learn how to become the absolute best version of yourself — to hold yourself to the highest standard of integrity and excellence — so that you can parent more effectively, lead by example, and become the kind of role model that your child needs and deserves?

If not, close this book right now. It will probably just bore or annoy you.

If your answer is "YES," keep reading.

You are about to begin a journey of self-evolution that can impact you and your child in profound and beautiful ways.

Why self-evolution?

Because as you grow, evolve, and create positive changes in your own life, you will naturally create positive changes in your child's life.

After all, you can't teach what you haven't learned.

You can't be a role model for something you don't currently practice.

If you want to teach your child to be trustworthy and reliable, then you need to be trustworthy and reliable.

If you want to teach your child to treat his or her body with respect, then you need to treat your own body with respect.

And so on, and so on, for every single value and lesson you hope to instill in your child.

Here is the good (no, GREAT!) news:

It is never too late to become the kind of person that you want to be — so that your child can have the kind of parent that he or she needs.

Never too late. No matter what.

If you are willing, the journey begins right here and now on this very page.

I am so glad you're (still) reading, and still here.

HOW THIS BOOK IS ORGANIZED AND WHAT TO READ FIRST

This book contains twenty chapters.

Each chapter dives into a particular struggle that many parents face — from dealing with a child who won't follow rules, do chores, or cooperate (Chapter One), to helping a child who is overweight to slim down in a healthy way (Chapter Eight), to parenting effectively when you are sick, exhausted, burned-out, struggling with addiction, or otherwise "not at your best" (Chapter Twenty).

In each chapter, you will find true stories from parents I have known and coached and / or counseled (all names and identifying details have been changed for privacy, of course).

You will find self-reflection questions to answer on your own, with your co-parent, and sometimes along with your child.

You will find tips and guidelines to help you set a beautiful example for your children and to parent more effectively.

Nothing in this book is "guesswork" or "theory." Everything in this book is grounded in my 29 years of combined experience as a psychologist, life coach, and attorney in the area of family law. I can't promise that my guidelines will solve everything for you, instantly and perfectly, but I can promise you this:

Your child may not necessarily give you this impression, but he or she is looking to you for guidance on how to function in the world. That guidance starts at home — with firm, fair, consistent rules applied with love — along with consequences for non-compliance.

Everyone needs a role model. Your child is no exception. And you are the most influential force in your child's life.

So, if you commit to living your life with integrity, fairness, and self-respect, then your child will be far more likely to follow in your shoes.

But your child cannot follow in your footsteps until you take the first step.

It starts with you.

As for "how to pace yourself as you read this book," here's my suggestion:

You can read this book all the way through, in order, cover to cover.

Or you can flip around and start with the chapter titles and topics that speak most strongly to you.

I do, however, highly recommend reading Chapter One before you progress onto any other chapters.

This is because Chapter One includes some basic information on how to set age-appropriate rules for your child, how to choose appropriate consequences, why enforcing consequences consistently is so important, how to create visual "charts" to track your child's behavior and keep him or her on track, and other fundamental techniques that form the basis for the rest of the book.

If you are wondering: "What age child does this book apply to? Is the book for children of all ages, or for children of specific ages?

My answer is: this book can be relevant to children of all ages in the sense that it is never too late to become the person, parent, and role model that you want to be.

And, even if you're already doing a pretty stellar job at parenting, it is never too late to learn how to do even better. As the late author Dr. Maya Angelou (and Oprah's mentor) so aptly said: "I did then what I knew how to do. Now that I know better, I do better."

At the end of this book, you will find a sample chart, an additional worksheet, a conversation script, and resources —

including the option for one-on-one coaching if that's something you'd like to explore.

However you choose to digest the materials in this book, I am sending you a tremendous wave of love and encouragement.

Parenting is big, important work and just by opening this book, you are proving that you are eager to meet the challenge — and give it your absolute best.

Let's begin…

THE BASICS

There is a lot of information in this guidebook — lots of stories, lots of dilemmas, lots of ideas for how to resolve common issues and create more peace at home.

As you read along, you may find yourself getting a bit overwhelmed, or perhaps even feeling like it's "just too late" to change your child's attitude or behavior.

That is not the case.

It is never too late to make a positive impact in a child's life — or in a grown up's life for that matter. With the right guidance, support, and systems in place, people of all ages can — and do — change.

But if you do find yourself feeling disheartened or overwhelmed, you can return to this section — which I call, THE BASICS — for a quick summary-list of all of the "big concepts" contained in this book.

My hope is that the following list will offer you some peace of mind and encouragement, reminding you that while parenting can often be challenging and demanding, that doesn't mean it has to be "mysterious" or "complicated."

It's actually pretty simple:

Be a good role model. Lead by example. It all starts with you.

Without further ado…

Here is a summary of the big, overarching concepts ("The Basics") to keep in mind as you read through this book:

1. You are your child's primary role model. It's natural for your child to look up to you, mimic you, and follow in your footsteps. Which means…

2. You cannot expect your child to behave in a way that you do not behave. If you want your child to change his or her habits (say, spending less time on the computer, being more patient, being more organized and responsible, eating more nutritious foods) then you must change your habits first.

3. "Talking" to your child is rarely enough to create a permanent change. Conversations can be a good starting point, but conversations alone rarely influence children's decisions. Supervision, rules and consequences do.

4. Your child is not likely to listen to you or cooperate if he or she does not trust you (because, for example, you've been unreliable or inconsistent in the past). If you can earn your child's trust, then he or she is more likely to follow your guidance.

5. Your parenting approach is not born "out of nowhere." As you parent your own child, you are probably emulating your own parents (consciously or unconsciously trying to be "just like them") or rebelling against your own parents (consciously or unconsciously trying to "not be like them").

In either scenario, it's valuable to do some self-reflection to better understand who you are, how your beliefs were formed, and to heal any parts of you that are still emotionally bruised from your own childhood, so that you don't bruise your children emotionally, too.

6. Setting rules — and applying consequences when your child chooses not to comply with the rules — does not make you "mean" or "unfair." It makes you an effective teacher, helping your child to learn important lessons about how the world works. (Read Chapter One for important information on how to set age-appropriate rules and consequences.)

7. Charts are your best friend. Use visual charts to spell out the rules and general requirements that you have for your child's behavior, as well as the consequences for not complying with the rules. Have your child use checkmarks, stickers or gold stars to mark down what's been followed and completed each day. Review your child's chart daily. If something gets missed, ask your child,

"What is the consequence for that?" This encourages your child to develop self-reliance and personal responsibility. (Flip to pages 158-165 for a sample chart along with a few more instructions on how to use charts effectively.)

8. Whenever possible, make sure that all of the role models in your child's life (parents, sitters, tutors, teachers, etc.) are on the same page, sharing the same values, and "in the know" about the rules and consequences that you've outlined. Present a "unified front" so that your child has no opportunity to become manipulative or seek out the more "lenient" adult when he or she wants to do something that's off limits.

9. Children are not born rude, defiant, insolent, greedy, selfish, etc. These are "learned behaviors." Which means (good news!) they can be unlearned, too.

10. It is never too late to make positive changes. When you begin to enforce new rules consistently, you may be surprised at how quickly your child adapts and gets on board. But, as always: being an admirable, inspiring role model is vital.

It always starts with you.

CHAPTER ONE

"My child won't cooperate!"

Christie is ready to explode.

"No matter what I say, my seven-year-old won't cooperate! He's behaving like a little monster. I don't know what to do."

"OK. Let's start with rules. Do you have clear rules for behavior? Does your son know what those rules are?"

Christie's eyebrows knit together, thinking deeply. Finally she says:

"Yes. I think so. We've got rules. I mean, my son isn't stupid. He's very smart. He knows how he is supposed to behave."

I scan her expression, which is telling me everything that she's not comfortable saying:

"... Except maybe our household rules aren't actually that clear..."

"What about consequences? When your son breaks a rule, do you implement consequences for misbehavior every single time? Some of the time? None of the time?"

Christie shoots me a guilty look that says, "Some or none of the time." Bingo. I know we've just arrived at the crux of the issue. Finally, she speaks again.

"Suzanne, I just hate punishing him. I hate saying 'no' to him. It just makes his behavior even worse. Tantrums, things like that. It breaks my heart to watch him screaming, so upset like that. One time, he actually said, 'I hate you, Mommy!'"

Hate. Such a harsh, terrible word for any parent to hear. My heart aches for Christie.

She's in a difficult position, indeed.

But there's hope. A great deal of hope, actually.

As a parent, you <u>can</u> take action to get your child back on track — at any time.

You don't have to think about this as "punishing" your child, but rather, applying "positive discipline" to educate your child about the difference between right and wrong.

What is "positive discipline"?

It means:

- Setting age-appropriate rules for your child.
- Explaining those rules so that your child understands why they are important.
- Enforcing those rules consistently. (Emphasis on: "consistently.")
- Applying consequences when rules get broken. Consistently. (Did I mention "consistently"?)

Of course, bringing positive discipline into your parenting is not always "easy" to do — especially if it is not something you've practiced before.

To begin this first chapter, I want you to understand why it's so important to set, explain and implement rules — and why doing so doesn't make you a "mean parent," but rather, a strong, loving, and effective parent. The kind of parent your child really needs.

Why rules matter.

Imagine a pair of siblings who grow up, become adults, and have no concept of "right" and "wrong."

They lie and cheat on their taxes, because they've figured out how to "work the system."

They steal packets of gum from the store, because it's not like it's a big deal.

They eat poorly and treat their bodies carelessly, because nothing "bad" has happened so far, so they are in the clear!

No need to be responsible. Because... there are no consequences.

Except, of course, the consequences will arrive eventually.

They always do. That's how life works.

And when those consequences finally arrive — a scary IRS notice in the mail, an arrest for shoplifting, developing diabetes due to years of poor eating habits and excess weight — these adults will be completely unprepared for it. They won't know what to do next. They will have an extremely difficult road ahead. A lot of tough "repair work" to do — and they won't be equipped with the life skills or emotional tools to do it.

So much of this pain could have been prevented.

How?

If their parents had been able to do their job properly.

Don't mean to point finger or pass blame, but it's true.

If their parents had known how to set clear rules, if they had implemented those rules, and if they had applied consequences for misbehavior when their now adult children were young, then these adult children would have been far more likely to learn important life lessons about proper conduct, compliance and consequences.

If you only absorb 53 words from this entire book, let it be these:

Every time you implement a rule, you are preparing your child for a happy, successful adulthood.

You are teaching your child important lessons about the connection between "not behaving properly" and the "consequences" that follow.

This is not an act of "meanness." This is an act of care — an act of love.

Never forget that.

"But why does it feel so hard to implement 'the rules' sometimes?"

That's something a huge number of parents have asked me over the years.

It's a big question!

Throughout the rest of this chapter, I will show you what it looks like to set age-appropriate rules, how to communicate those rules to your child, how to implement those rules, and apply consequences for non-compliance.

Of course, as with every lesson you hope to teach to your child, it all starts with you!

Let's take a moment to explore why you might be struggling to set and implement rules.

Struggling to set rules, implement rules, and apply consequences?

Here's what that might mean about you:
It could mean that…

- Your parents were very strict, perhaps overly strict, and you don't want to be "restrictive" or "oppressive" like that to your own child.
- You're afraid that your child will think that you are "mean" and won't like you.
- You're afraid that rules will stifle your child's creativity and individuality.

Do any of these statements ring true?

Here's some good news: no matter how you were raised, and no matter what kind of parent you've been for your child so far (too lenient, too strict, inconsistent, overprotective, etc.) you can make changes and improvements. Starting today.

Step one? Choosing age-appropriate rules and consequences for your child.

Rules and consequences: what's appropriate for each age group?

You don't need to be a "parenting expert" to recognize that a three-year-old will not understand the connection between "behavior" and "consequences" in the same way that a thirteen-year-old will.

Which means that you know it's important to set "age-appropriate" rules and consequences based on your child's intellectual and emotional maturity level.

It's also important to choose consequences that are "in proportion" to your child's degree of misbehavior. Just like you wouldn't face a year in jail for running a red light, you don't want to ground your teenager for a year because he or she came home one hour after curfew!

If you're wondering what kinds of rules and consequences might be appropriate for your child, at your child's current age, the following guidelines can help.

Ages 0 to 2.

Children in this age group are a little too young to understand the concept of a "consequence" for misbehavior. Instead, I recommend that, when necessary, parents firmly but kindly and patiently keep repeating and reinforcing the word, "No."

("No, don't stand near the hot stove." "No, don't walk out that door." "No, don't touch that.")

Move down to your child's eye level — meaning, physically bend down and hold their little hands gently, but firmly — as you look them straight in the eye and say, "No."

Let your child experience "healthy fear" (aka: respect) for your authority ("Ooh, I don't want to mess with Mommy (or Daddy)!"). And of course: be sure to take basic safety precautions and childproof your home!

Why no "consequences" at this age? Because during this stage of development, your child is so naturally curious, wants to explore and touch everything, and simply doesn't know any better. By implementing consequences at this early age, you would be "punishing" your young child for… being a young child. Applying consequences would not be fair or appropriate.

Again: you are going to need to say a thousand "No's" as you teach your child what's acceptable to touch, explore and play with, and what is not.

It's important to say these "No's" calmly, patiently and firmly. Your little one's short-term memory is not yet developed. This means that they will need a lot of reminders.

Let's look at two common scenarios for children in this age range.

Throwing food.

To you, it's messy and annoying. But to your young child? It's just playful exploration.

Here's how to handle the situation: when your child starts throwing food, say, "No" in a calm, firm tone. Stop the meal, take him or her out of the chair and clean the food up together. "No." Stop. Clean up together. "No." Stop. Clean up together. Every time.

This is not a "consequence" per se, but you are still educating your child about what's appropriate behavior and what's not. Through your words, tone and actions, you are showing your child that throwing food is a no-no. Parents who consistently handle their children in this way have told me, repeatedly, that their children do get the message.

Screaming in public places.

When this happens, remove your child from the situation and go and sit in your car or in some other private space.

This can sometimes be inconvenient for you as the parent, but it's a way to let your child "cry it out" while giving you a chance to figure out if there is a problem that needs to be dealt with (like a soiled diaper) or if this is just an attention-seeking tantrum.

If it's a tantrum, then after your child has settled down, you can say, firmly but lovingly: "No, that was not acceptable." Your child may not fully grasp the meaning of your words, but based on your facial expression and tone, he or she is likely to get the message that screaming in public (or anywhere, for that matter) is not OK.

What if these approaches don't work?

If your crawling baby or rambunctious toddler does not comply, do not take your frustration out on them by spanking them or yelling angrily. Remember, you are a teacher. Good teachers are patient.

Good teachers also model the kind of behavior that they want their children to emulate.

So, keep your own room tidy, for example, and put things away in the kitchen. This way, you're more likely to see your little ones (age-appropriate) putting their things back where they belong — just like mommy / daddy does!

Ages 3 to 5.

Around this age, your child is old enough to begin to understand the link between "behavior" and a "consequence." So, this is an appropriate age to have your first "family meeting" where you explain the rules and the consequences for non-compliance.

It is critical that you introduce and explain the rules and the consequences clearly (for example: "No drawing on your bedroom walls with crayons. Crayons are only to be used on paper") <u>before</u> you impose a consequence (for example: "Now you can't use crayons for the rest of the day.").

With clear instructions, your child can begin to make an informed choice about how to behave. In time, he or she will most likely understand, "Oh, I get it. If I draw on my wall with my crayons, I won't be able to use my crayons for the rest of the day."

It's also a good idea to explain the <u>reason</u> for the rule — using a word like "because" (for example: "You can draw with your crayons on paper, but not on the walls, <u>because</u> crayons make marks on the walls, and that is not ok"). Don't just lay down the rule without any explanation. By explaining the reason for the rule, you're giving your child something to wrap their mind around, rather than having them blindly obey what you say.

To recap:

- Introduce the rule.
- Explain the reason for the rule.
- Identify the consequence that will follow if the rule is not followed. Not complying with the rule.

... all <u>before</u> applying a consequence for breaking the rule. (This explain-explain-explain guideline applies to children in this age group and older.)

By laying out everything clearly, in advance, you are giving your child a fair chance at making a good choice (which means complying and avoiding a consequence!).

Charts are your best friend.

One last note for children in this age group (and children who are older)...

I highly recommend creating some type of **"daily chart" system** to keep track of rules and responsibilities (for example: chores that need to get done, bath time, bed time, etc.) and what the consequences will be if your child does not comply.

Then, as your child completes each item, he or she should be instructed to check it off on the chart with a mark, a sticker, or a gold star — just like checking things off a grown-up "to-do list." This prevents any arguments about what has or hasn't been done and whether or not a particular consequence is "fair." It's all documented on the chart!

Flip to pages 158-165 for a sample chart along with a few more instructions on how to use charts effectively.

Ages 6 to 8.

By this age, most children are mature enough to understand the link between "behavior" and "consequences," especially if you've been instilling (and re-instilling) this lesson for several years already.

Of course, behavior issues may still arise. So, what's an appropriate type of consequence for children in this age bracket?

Many parents think that "time-outs" are a fair consequence for children in this age group. I suggest that time-outs be used only as a last resort. This is because time-outs, when properly implemented, are so restrictive — the child is essentially told to stare at a blank wall and do nothing. It is as if all of the child's rights have been temporarily taken away. That's a pretty extreme consequence for a six-year-old!

I suggest withdrawing other privileges first, before resorting to a time-out (for example: "If you don't put your clothes in the hamper, the consequence will be: you don't get to watch your favorite TV program tonight," or, "If you don't help tidy up and put your toys away after you finish playing, the consequence will be: you don't get to play at your friend's house after school tomorrow.").

Your child will <u>not</u> want to forfeit his or her favorite privileges. This means that your child will be motivated to behave properly so that they can keep the privilege.

Ultimately, of course, you want your child to behave properly because it is the "right" thing to do, not because they could lose a privilege.

However, the consequence serves as a motivator to help your child make better behavior choices. Once they're behaving more appropriately, then their mindset can shift from:

"I'm doing my chores because I don't want to miss the sleepover this weekend" to:

"I'm doing my chores, because that's my responsibility."

Ages 9 to 12.

By this age, children begin to understand that there are "natural" consequences for non-compliance (for example: "If I don't do my homework, I might get a poor grade") as well as "parental-imposed" consequences for non-compliance (for example: "If I don't do my homework, I won't be allowed to watch my favorite TV show.").

Many parents think that if children experience a natural consequence, that's "enough" of a consequence for them to realize that they need to change their behavior.

I disagree.

In my work with parents, I have found that children still need parental-imposed consequences, not just natural ones, in order for certain lessons to fully sink in. Natural consequences, alone, are not strong enough motivators for children in this age group.

As an example: one of my clients was a father with an eleven-year-old son. His son had not finished his homework, and instead, was watching TV after dinner. The father believed that the child should suffer the consequences of getting a bad grade in order to "learn his lesson."

A better option, in my opinion, would be to instruct the eleven-year-old to go to bed early, get up earlier than usual the next morning (when he's more rested), and finish his homework so that he can turn it in on time. Then, a parental-imposed consequence ought to be imposed (for example: "You can't use your iPad today.").

This allows the child to avoid an unnecessary problem that could hinder his future success (getting a bad grade) yet he's still being taught an important lesson: homework must come first or certain privileges, like TV and electronics, get taken away.

To use a different example: if your daughter went to bed without brushing her teeth, would you want her to get a cavity (a natural consequence) to "teach her a lesson" about dental hygiene? No, of course not. It would be better to instruct her to get out of bed, brush her teeth properly, and then get back into bed — while removing a privilege in the process ("No video games tomorrow because you didn't brush your teeth."). This allows your child to learn a valuable lesson ("brushing my teeth is important!") without incurring damaging consequences ("cavities") in the learning process.

Ages 13 and older.

Depending on the degree of your child's misbehavior, and whether this is the first time the rules have been violated, or a repeated issue, an appropriate consequence could be: getting grounded for a weekend, a week or a month; no cell phone privileges for a weekend, a week or a month; or an earlier bedtime or curfew.

To reiterate some of my earlier suggestions: when your child chooses not to comply with a rule, it's important for you to temporarily take away one of your child's <u>favorite privileges</u> (just like if you violate the rules of the road, you may need to forfeit the privilege of your driver's license for a period of time).

Explain to your child that they need to earn their lost privilege back by complying with the rules you've set (just like you need to attend traffic school and comply with the rules of your suspended license in order to earn back your driving privileges).

For example: if your teenage son does poorly in school because he repeatedly fails to turn in homework assignments on time, then his electronics privileges may be forfeited for the semester, and potentially longer if his grades for that semester do not improve.

Implementing a consequence for misbehavior prepares your child for "real life" (aka: grown up life) in the future.

A driver's license, a rental agreement for an apartment, a credit card — all these items are privileges. If we don't follow the rules associated with those privileges (follow the rules of the road, abide by the terms of our rental agreement and pay our rent on time, make timely card payments), we run the risk of losing those privileges and we would need to earn them back.

Teach your child that "when you misbehave, there is always a consequence: a privilege gets taken away and you must earn it back."

This, in my opinion, is one of the most important lessons you can teach your child.

Take every possible opportunity to be a firm but loving educator.

Your child might grumble and fuss now, but one day? Your child will thank you for it.

A few recommendations and reminders for ALL age groups:

- *Closely monitor your child's behavior to nip misbehavior in the bud.*

If you notice a rule violation, you can allow for a brief "grace period" while your child adjusts to the new rule (in some cases, he or she may have truly just "forgotten" about the new rule — we'll discuss that in a moment).

But after one or two violations, then apply the consequence that you've explained to your child in advance.

- *Be consistent and get all the caregivers on board.*

If you're not able to be present — say, when you're at work — then make sure that whoever is supervising your child in your absence shares your values and is "in the know" about the rules.

It's so much easier to raise responsible children when all of the caregivers in your child's life are on the same page.

For example, if you don't allow your child to eat ice cream before dinner, but the babysitter does, then your child may give you a hard time when you tell them, "No chocolate ice cream before dinner." You're likely to hear, "But [insert name of babysitter] lets us have ice cream before dinner!" or, "Aunt Rose lets us stay up past bedtime," or "Uncle Bob let's us watch TV while we're eating dinner" and so on.

- *Charts, charts, charts. Love them. Use them.*

As I mentioned earlier in this chapter, it's a great idea to create a daily chart with rules and responsibilities, and a section to mark that a particular task is "done" to track your child's behavior. The chart should also indicate what the consequence will be if something doesn't get "done" or isn't followed.

At the end of each day, sit down with your child and review the chart. For younger children (ages 4 to 7), you can initiate the meeting. With older children (ages 8 and up) instruct them to bring their chart to you each evening. Make it clear that it is their responsibility to initiate this "chart review" session nightly. If they don't, apply a consequence.

The beauty of using a chart system is that it's black and white. No debating, arguing or lecturing is necessary because everything is documented on the chart. If your child violates a rule or does not complete an assigned chore, ask them: "What is the consequence for that?" If they say they don't know, you can point to the consequence that's written on the chart.

- *Use a calm tone, even when your child misbehaves.*

If your child violates a rule, resist the urge to yell or speak angrily. You don't need to scream, "Now you're grounded this weekend!" or "No phone for you today!"

Try to use a calm, firm, matter of fact tone, asking, "What is the consequence for what you just did?" and then wait for your child to respond.

This takes all the anger and animosity out of the situation and helps your child to connect the dots between "behavior" and "consequence," without casting you as the "angry villain" in the story. Let the consequence speak for itself (and for you!). No additional "anger" is required to get the point across.

"What if my child messes up once or twice? Should I let it slide or enforce a consequence every single time?"

Up to around age six, you can give your child a couple of "tries" to adapt to the new rule.

The first time your child doesn't follow the rule, matter-of-factly reiterate the rule and the consequence. The same goes for the second time. After the third time, apply a consequence. Why three tries? Because at this young age, your child's short-term memory isn't fully in place yet. By giving three attempts, you are giving your child a fair chance to practice and get it right.

For ages seven and above, I'd suggest giving one try to learn the new behavior, not two. If your child doesn't follow the rule for a second time, then say, "Now what is the consequence for what you just did?" Have your child tell you. (Resist the urge to tell them what the consequence is. It's valuable for your child to say it out loud.)

"How much 'reminding' should I do?"

Up to around age six, you could spend a few minutes at the beginning of each day reviewing the rules on the "chart" for the day, until your child has got the required behavior down pat.

For ages seven and above, during the first few days after you first introduce the "chart" you could review it with your child at the beginning of the day. After that, it's your child's responsibility to remember what to do.

If you are constantly reminding your child all day long ("Hey, it's time to pick up your toys," "Remember: do your homework before playing computer games," and so on) that is counter-productive. Your child needs to learn that it's important to take personal responsibility for his or her behavior rather than relying on somebody else to continually "chime in" with helpful reminders.

If you sense that your child is slipping, you can intervene, but let your child tell <u>you</u> what needs to be done.

You could say something like, "Please get your chart and tell me what you need to remember to do today." Let your child provide the answers. This gets him or her thinking and actively engaged in the conversation, instead of passively listening to you "lecturing" or "nagging" about what needs to be done and behaviors that are required.

"I've tried consequences, but they don't 'work' for my child."

That's something I hear often!
Here are four questions that I ask parents in this situation:

1. Are you applying the consequences consistently?
The answer is often a sheepish "no" or "yes, but..." or "well, kind of..."
Consistency is essential in order for consequences to be effective.
Try becoming much, much more consistent before you decide that consequences "don't work" for your child.

2. Is everyone on the same page?
Sometimes, other caregivers (babysitters, co-parents, grandparents) aren't "in the know" about what the rules and consequences are, or are not enforcing them in your absence. That's a problem. It's time for you to be a leader and get everyone on the same page for the wellbeing and benefit of your child.

3. Did you create a chart system?
Charts can work miracles because — as I've emphasized a number of times already! — they put a quick end to arguments and debates about "fairness." When you're using a daily chart system, nothing is vague and everything is "in writing," so to speak.
If your child completes a chore (or follows a rule), they get a checkmark or a gold star. If your child doesn't fully comply with the chart? No check, no star, and you have an opportunity to ask your child, "What is the consequence for what you did / did not do?"
(Again: you can flip to pages 158-165 in this book for a sample chart that you can Xerox, tear out, or use as a general model for your own homemade, artistic chart-masterpiece! — along with a few more instructions on how to use charts effectively).

4. *What kinds of consequences are you applying? Are they strong enough?*

Consequences tend to be most effective when you are temporarily removing one of your child's favorite privileges — like TV, video games, cell phone use, sleepovers, playtime with friends, and so on.

If you are choosing a consequence that is not "strong" enough (or too strong), your child won't have much motivation to comply.

Make these four adjustments and you may discover that, in fact, consequences really do "work" quite well!

"What about giving rewards for good behavior?"

It's not uncommon for parents to offer their children a reward to get them to comply with a rule ("If you tidy you room, then I'll take you to the movies.") But this is not a reward — it's a bribe.

"Bribery" is not an effective parenting technique. All you're doing is setting your child up to always want "something" in exchange for good behavior, rather than behaving properly because it is the appropriate, responsible, "right" thing to do.

When you rely on bribes to motivate your child, then the next time you ask your eight-year-old to clear the dishes off the dinner table, don't be surprised if she responds with, "How much will you pay me?" (Shockingly, this actually happened to one of my clients!)

If your child's behavior improves, you can absolutely praise him or her ("Great job!" "Look at all those gold stars on your chart!" "Keep up the good work!"), but resist the urge to start doling out treats and rewards left and right. That's not how life works. We don't receive a blue ribbon just for showing up to work on time. "Rewards" should be reserved for extraordinary achievements — not everyday chores and compliance.

Here's an example of a scenario when giving a special reward would be appropriate:

Let's say your daughter works tremendously hard on a school project. She goes "above and beyond" the assignment and earns an A+ for her efforts. In that instance, you might acknowledge her extra effort by saying, "I know how hard you worked on this project and I'm so proud of you. So let's go and buy you that sweater you've been wanting."

Closing words: Christie's happy ending.

Christie — the mom with the rule-breaking, tantrum-throwing seven-year-old who would not cooperate — returned to my office a few weeks after our initial conversation.

During that time, we'd had several follow up phone sessions to continue our work together.

We focused on outlining age-appropriate rules and identifying appropriate consequences for her young child.

I challenged her to enforce these new rules consistently, even when her son threw a tantrum or resisted this new system.

I also encouraged her to explain to her son,

"If you throw a tantrum about these rules or talk back or are sassy, then there will be a consequence for that, too."

I reminded her that implementing consequences is not "mean." It's actually an act of deep love. A gift for her child. She promised she would do what we discussed — and she did.

When I saw her again, she was glowing with pride and relief.

"It worked!" she exclaimed. "My son was <u>not</u> happy about my new parenting style," she laughed. "But I am already seeing a shift in his behavior. I feel like he respects me more. He's behaving. He even seems happier and more confident. He's listening to me."

I congratulated her on her success.

And yes, I see this kind of "happy ending" often. In many instances, it really <u>is</u> possible to re-direct your child's behavior, no matter how rocky things have gotten.

When you step fully into your role as a parent — a source of unconditional love, but also a source of clear rules and unflinching boundaries — that is when you give your child the best possible chance at success.

There may be some initial resistance, but with time, firm and loving guidance, and consistency, — that is how you give your child's behavior the best possible chance to shift.

Lead by example. Begin today.

Through your own behavior, every day, show your child what it looks like to make good choices, to behave responsibly and respectfully, and to do what is right.

Show your child the benefits of making these kinds of choices and living this way: benefits like happiness, success, and peace of mind.

Phew!

That wraps up Chapter One — definitely the longest, meatiest chapter of this book, but packed with a lot of important information that will inform our discussions going forward.

From here, go ahead and move along to Chapter Two, or whatever chapter title and topic calls out to you!

CHAPTER TWO

"My child is so manipulative! He's always playing one parent against the other."

Cindy and Joe came to see me because of Cindy's concern that their eight-year-old son was "manipulative."

Joe thought Cindy was making too much of a fuss about this, but agreed to come along to the coaching session because he wants to be a good dad to his son — and a good partner to his wife.

"Our son Mike plays violent video games even when I've told him not to," Cindy tells me. "I've caught him sneaking into the den to play a game when he thinks I won't notice. He has become secretive and dishonest. When I ask him why he disobeys me, he says, 'Dad doesn't mind! I was being quiet so I thought you wouldn't catch me doing it'."

Upon hearing this, I wanted to know more about how Mike had learned to manipulate and use dad against mom to get his way.

So I asked both parents, "It sounds like the two of you aren't on the same page when it comes to parenting your son, or at least when it come to video games. Am I right?"

Cindy jumped right in, as if she'd been bursting to share how her husband overrode her parenting decisions.

"Joe knows I don't want our eight-year-old playing video games that are graphic and violent, but he buys them anyway. He says all of Mike's friends play these games. We get into big blowouts over this, which Mike usually overhears. The outcome is always the same — Mike gets to keep his game and Dad gets his way."

Yikes. Not too difficult to identify the crux of the issue, now is it?

It's a real problem when parents override each other — and Mike is a prime example of what can happen when parents disagree or have conflicting values. Mike has learned to manipulate and use one parent against the other so he can do what he wants.

So, what's the solution?

Obviously, both parents must come to an agreement so that they can present a "unified front" for their child.

But in order to do this, a bit of self-reflection is often necessary.

If your spouse or co-parent tends to be "super strict" and you tend to be more "super lenient," or vice versa, both of you may want to examine why that's the case.

For example, if Joe never got to do what he wanted to do as a child and he experienced a lot of harsh "NO's!" from his parents, or perhaps screaming and yelling in his home (instead of parents who patiently explained why he couldn't always do what he wanted to do) then it would not be uncommon for someone like Joe, as an adult, to resist rules and structure and want to be an "easy-going dad" for his own child.

In other words: Joe might be "compensating" for his own unhappy childhood by making sure his child doesn't experience the same rigidity and oppressive atmosphere that he did. This doesn't mean that Joe is a "bad dad," by any means. But by recognizing where his parenting approach is coming from (in this instance, his own childhood), Joe may be able to find a healthier, more balanced parenting style.

Self-reflection.

If you're wanting to course-correct a child who is manipulative, dishonest, or cleverly seeking out the more "lenient" parent in order to get what he or she wants, here are a few questions to ask yourself.

These questions can help you see how your upbringing, your past, and your personal choices may have contributed to creating this situation...

- Were my parents very strict? Or overly lenient?
- Was I ever allowed to do what I wanted as a child? Or was I always told "NO!"?
- Do I feel like my parents stifled my creativity or originality?
- Did I frequently see one or both of my parents arguing about the rules or overriding the other's wishes?
- Do I still feel "emotionally bruised" from my own childhood?
- Do I want my child to have more freedom and privileges than I had?

If you answered "Yes" to any of the questions above, have empathy for yourself because of what you experienced as a child.

It's OK if you're still mad. It's OK if you're still hurt. It doesn't mean that your parents were "bad" people. In all likelihood, they were doing the best that they could with the tools, skills, and knowledge that they had at the time. But that doesn't mean that when it comes to parenting, they gave you everything that you needed — and deserved.

Even so, for the benefit of your child, it's important to release any emotional baggage towards your parents that you may be holding onto, even if it's just a teensy little carry-on bag.

Either out loud or inside your own mind, trying saying to yourself:

"That was then, this is now.
I am no longer that young child being subjected to [whatever you experienced that bruised your feelings].
I can begin to heal that part of me that still feels emotionally bruised, by being empathetic and understanding."

Imagine that you are speaking directly to your inner child.

Imagine that you can "re-parent" that smaller, younger version of yourself.

Imagine that you can give that part of yourself everything your parents didn't or couldn't.

Try saying:

"Younger Self, I'm sorry your parents were [strict / unfair / overbearing / overly lenient / whatever parenting behavior comes to mind].

But I am your parent now. I am the grown up in charge now.

I love you and I won't ever let you experience that again."

By healing the child within, you are allowing the tender, emotionally bruised parts of yourself to mend. This can help you to feel more emotionally mature and to become an even more solid, effective parent for your own child today.

(And by the way, this goes for parents on both ends of the spectrum: parents who have a tendency to be overly lenient, and parents who have a tendency to be excessively strict. And if you're engaging in any other kind of behavior that's causing friction or disagreement with your spouse or co-parent, it's a good idea to examine — and heal — that part of yourself.)

"What if my spouse or co-parent and I just CANNOT agree?"

It is so destructive for your child to see you and your spouse or co-parent "battling it out."

It can make your child feel uneasy and unsafe. Which means that your child is more likely to "act out" by breaking rules, throwing tantrums, or engaging in defiant behavior that mimics the same kind of hostility your child is witnessing in the two of you.

Imagine watching a televised broadcast from the White House where the President and the Secretary of Defense are dead-locked in a bitter feud, in total opposition over an important military decision. Seeing that probably wouldn't inspire feelings of "trust," "admiration" or "security," would it? Depending on what the

President and Secretary are arguing over, you might actually feel really scared!

Instead of battling in front of your child, hash out your differences behind closed doors.

Let go of the "my way is the right way" mentality.

Instead, focus on what's truly best for your child.

If the two of you find yourselves caught in a power struggle over parenting issues, take a time-out to breathe for a few seconds so that both of you can calm down. Then, each of you needs to ask yourself: "What would be best for my child right now?"

The answer to that question will point both of you towards your next move.

I also suggest that each of you take some time to write down your goals for raising your child (how you want your child to behave, the values you wish to instill, what is acceptable behavior and what's not).

Do this goal-writing exercise separately. Then, agree on a time when you will meet and read your lists out loud to each other. Agree that you will listen patiently to what each other has to say without interrupting or jumping in.

Discuss what each of you wrote on your lists and then compile a new parenting plan based on your two lists. A plan that both of you can agree on. A plan that reflects your current beliefs and values — not a plan that is "in reaction" to your upbringing or the past.

When you take a team approach to parenting, you will have a much better chance at bringing out the best in your child. Present a unified front, and your child is less likely to have the desire (or the opportunity!) to lie, manipulate, or go behind anyone's back to get what he or she wants.

Closing words: Resolution and unity, at last.

Cindy, Joe and I had several follow-up phone sessions after our initial conversation.

It quickly became apparent that they were not only "at odds" over violent video games, they were battling over just about everything — bedtimes, dress code, playdates, meals, you name it!

I worked with Cindy and Joe on learning to resolve their disagreements by improving their communication skills — by talking, listening and respecting each other's point of view instead of leaping into combat-mode.

I also pointed out how healthy it would be for their son to see them communicate calmly and reach compromises. Initially, Joe was a bit resistant. But he really wanted to be the best dad he could be, and he promised to focus on improving his communication skills — and he did.

I also helped these parents to understand that setting rules and applying consequences is actually a priceless gift for their child — just like we talked about in Chapter One of this book. I recommended that they post the rules and consequences for misbehavior in a visible place, like on the refrigerator, so that their son Mike would know exactly what was required of him.

One month later, when these parents returned to see me in my office, it was heartwarming to hear that their parenting problems were improving significantly.

"Our communication has improved," said Cindy. Joe chimed in, "And we're fighting less."

"And," said Cindy, beaming with pride, "we reached an agreement that Mike can play video games after he finishes his homework, but not violent ones. We're choosing his games together and we're both happy with that compromise."

They also reported that Mike was becoming a lot more cooperative across the board, not just when it came to video games. "He's behaving so much better," said Joe. "It's amazing! He doesn't want any consequences so he's motivated to follow the rules."

I encouraged them to continue being consistent — which means sticking closely to the rules they have set up and implementing consequences as needed.

I'm happy to report that these parents are succeeding. Mike's manipulative maneuvering — pitting his parents against each other and siding with his dad because he is the one who favors Mike's demands — has become a non-issue.

CHAPTER THREE

*"My child is an underachiever.
Why won't he reach his potential?"*

Kevin, age eleven, is a smart child who achieves high scores on intelligence tests.

Unfortunately, his grades at school are very poor.

His parents have tried everything they can think of. Frustrated, and reaching their wit's end, they hire me for coaching.

During our initial session, I learn that Kevin tends to be disorganized and doesn't always finish his homework or turn it in. Kevin tends to blame others for his poor productivity ("My teacher gives us too much homework!" or "The assignment is too hard, it's unfair!").

Kevin's mother has tried to encourage him to apply himself, but so far she's been unsuccessful.

She tells me, "I tell Kevin he can improve, if he'd only try. I've even had him evaluated by a learning specialist," she tells me.

Kevin's dad is frustrated and vents to his wife, "I don't understand what's wrong with him — his cousin gets A's, and you always did well in school."

They've both spoken to Kevin's teacher, who thinks that Kevin has low self-esteem. She told them, "Kevin thinks he's not good at anything, so he doesn't try because he's afraid of failing."

Based on the nuggets of information I've gotten, I already suspect that Kevin's teacher is right on the mark.

That's because it's common for underachieving children, like Kevin, to have low self-esteem. When you lack confidence in yourself, it feels preferable to "do nothing" (not do your homework assignment, skip class, miss the test, drop off the sports team) rather than risk failing and possibly being made fun of by your peers or disappointing your parents.

What causes a child to develop low self-esteem?

There are lots of factors that can contribute to this situation, but ultimately, it can invariably be traced back to you, your spouse / co-parent or both of you. (And by extension possibly tracing back through the generations to your own parents, for example, and their parents, and so forth.)

When Rick, Kevin's dad, was a child, his father would try to help him with his homework. Rick remembers his dad being very impatient.

"When I made mistakes, Dad got very frustrated and called me stupid!"

This damaged Rick's self-esteem. Lacking the confidence he needed to succeed, he did poorly in school.

As an adult, Rick continues to be a bit of an underachiever. He often remarks, "I do just enough at work to get by" — these types of comments are overheard by Kevin.

Following his father's example, Kevin performs far below his potential.

Here are a few other scenarios that can contribute to low self-esteem:

If you push your children too hard, constantly pressuring them to excel, they can develop low self-esteem because they may feel like, "I will never be good enough to please Mom / Dad."

If you are too "helpful" and overprotective, constantly assisting your child with his or her homework, for example, then your child may develop low self-esteem because he or she feels like, "I'm a loser, I can't do anything on my own."

Whatever the source of a child's low self-esteem may be, it is possible to turn the tide around.

With a few adjustments to your parenting approach, self-confidence can be strengthened.

It's never too late for children (or grown ups, for that matter) to learn how to like, respect and trust themselves.

Self-reflection.

If your child is performing below his or her potential, here are a few questions that can help you to see how your past, your upbringing, and your current beliefs may have contributed to this situation...

- Were my parents impatient with me when I made mistakes?
- Did my parents criticize and judge me when I got things wrong?
- Did my parents compare me to others who did things "better" than me? (For example: "Why can't you be more like your sister?")
- Did my parents expect me to excel, always, no matter what?
- Did my parents only treat me, hug me or praise me when I had done something extraordinary?
- Were my parents overprotective? Maybe "too helpful"? Always trying to "help" me with homework, projects, or contests, to "make sure" that I'd be the best?
- Were my parents inconsistent in their parenting approaches and opinions? (For example: one parent said, "You can quit the swim team, no big deal," while the other said, "No, you made a commitment and you must keep it.")

If you answered "Yes" to any of these questions, then it's possible that your self-esteem may have been bruised as a child. This lingering "bruising" may be influencing your parenting style — and your own child — today.

Finding solutions.

If your child is struggling with low self-esteem… what's your first step?
Parent: heal thyself.
Improving your child's self-esteem and self-confidence starts with you.

- *Are you fixated on being "perfect"*

If so, can you find it within yourself to let go of that need for control and perfectionism — for your own benefit and also for your child? Can you do your best and let that be good enough?

- *Or, conversely, are you underperforming at your job?*

If so, can you address that, and show your child that it is possible to transform, reach higher, and do better?

- *Does a part of you still feel scared about "failing," making you hesitant to even try to reach for your full potential?*

If so, can you speak kindly and tenderly to that bruised part of yourself, offering words of reassurance? Try saying:

"I love you for who you are, not for what you achieve."

Or:

"Trying is beautiful no matter what the final outcome may be. If you try, and really give your personal best, then you can feel proud of yourself. You're a champion."

One day, hopefully soon, you'll be able to say these same words to your own child — and really mean them.
But you will not be able to offer loving words of reassurance, effectively, until you can give that same reassurance to yourself first.
Begin by strengthening your own self-esteem so that you can model healthy self-confidence for your child.

Closing words: Aiming for "excellence" not "perfection."

After several meetings with me, Kevin's father had a big realization.

"When I criticize Kevin," Rick said, "He feels worse about himself than he already does. Just like my dad did with me. So now, I don't judge Kevin when he doesn't do so well at school. I ask him why he thinks it's happening. I listen. We try to solve this together."

Rick also realized that he needed to stop comparing Kevin to his cousin ("Why can't you get good grades like Allison does?") and to his mother ("Your mother did well in school").

As I explained to this dad, "Comparisons are crushing to children who are struggling academically — they feel pressured to live up to other people's standards, something they may not be able to do."

I encouraged Kevin's parents to create an organizational system that could set their son up for greater success — using a chart to track assignments and chores. I explained, "These organizational skills can help Kevin to be more successful in school and in life."

I also urged these parents to supervise Kevin's studies, monitoring closely to make sure he's completing his work as required.

The goal: to apply "parental consequences" to guide his behavior in the right direction ("Since you chose not to complete your assignment, you'll have to stay home this weekend to finish it instead of playing with your friends") while helping Kevin to avoid "natural consequences" that could hinder his success (like getting held back when his classmates move onto the next grade level).

(Review Chapter One for more details on "parental" versus "natural" consequences. It's an important topic to grasp.)

Nowadays, Kevin's parents praise him when he makes progress. If there's no improvement, they try to help him identify why he isn't progressing, and resolve the problem together.

This loving, caring attentiveness has boosted Kevin's confidence. I am happy to report: he's doing much better in school.

CHAPTER FOUR

"My child is so stressed all the time. Why is she such a perfectionist?"

Abby's mother came to see me because she was concerned about her thirteen-year-old's emotional health and wellbeing.

"It may look like Abby has everything going for her. She's incredibly hardworking and she gets straight A's at school," her mother tells me. "But I'm worried about her."

I ask her to elaborate.

Abby's mom explains that when Abby makes a mistake, she's not just upset — she's devastated. When there's an exam coming up, Abby panics. She doesn't sleep enough, she skips meals and doesn't socialize with her friends.

The school counselor is becoming concerned, too. The counselor says that Abby recently told her that, "All that matters is getting A's."

What causes this kind of "overachieving" tendency to arise?

The surprising reality is that overachievers, like Abby, often suffer from low self-esteem — just like underachievers, which we discussed in the previous chapter.

Underachievers perform below their ability because they don't believe they are "good enough" or capable of succeeding. They choose not to try at all, rather than risk failure.

Overachievers push themselves to the breaking point for the same reason — they don't believe they are "good enough" or capable of succeeding. They choose to overstudy, overreach, and over-prepare rather than risk failure.

Overachievers also feel compelled to achieve, achieve, achieve, and achieve some more because they need assurance that they're "worth" something. They tend to measure their value by what they achieve — which can be crushing, because when they slip up, even the tiniest bit, it's like their self-worth has been extinguished.

What's the greatest lesson you can teach an overachieving child?

"Let go of needing to be the best, all the time. Just do your best."

Self-reflection.

Does your child have overachieving tendencies that are hindering his or her happiness, health and success?

Here are a few questions to help you see how your upbringing, your past, and your personal choices might have contributed to creating this situation…

You can also use some of these questions as a starting point for a conversation with your child (see: my suggestions below).

- *Did my parents always expect (or push) me to be "the best"?*

(If so, you may be repeating the dynamic you experienced as a child.)

- *Was I the "black sheep" of the family? The weird one, or the underachiever, or the one who never "got it right," amidst a family of high achievers?*

(If so, then you might be compensating by wanting your child to be what you weren't able to be: "the best." You might be living your unmet dreams through your child.)

- *Was I afraid of not pleasing my parents when I was a child? Did I feel guilty if I disappointed them?*

(If so, ask your child if he or she has the same fear and guilt.)

- *As a child, did I get scolded harshly if I made a mistake, didn't win, or didn't bring home straight A's?*

(If so, are you repeating that pattern with your own child?)

If, through this line of questioning, you discover there is a part of you that is still emotionally bruised from the past, you can talk to that part of yourself as if you are talking to an actual child.

Speak words of healing and reassurance.

Either out loud or inside your mind, try saying:

"Self, I am sorry you felt pressured to overachieve as a child.

I am sorry you didn't feel 'good enough' and that you felt like you had to push, push, and push harder to be worthy of love and respect.

But that's all in the past. There's nothing to be frightened about now.

It's ok to make mistakes. It's ok to try and not succeed instantly. It's ok to just be you.

You have nothing to fear. I will always love you and care for you."

By healing your inner child, you will be better equipped to parent your own child and help him or her to build up more self-esteem.

"But isn't being 'the best' a good thing?"

Being "the best" is wonderful — but nobody can be "the best" one hundred percent of the time.

Children (and grown ups) run into problems when their drive to be "the best" becomes an obsession, and begins to take a toll on their physical and / or emotional wellbeing.

Sometimes parents unintentionally pressure children to strive too much — and then fear of failure can drive these children to be compulsively productive, and to feel guilty if they're not "the best" at everything they do.

If your child feels pressured to excel, teach your child that "Your 'worth' as a human being isn't defined by what you do," and that "You are special no matter what you do or don't accomplish."

Show your child that a "drive to achieve" can be fueled by a healthy desire for success (reaching your "personal best") not by fear and guilt.

Of course, to be an effective teacher, you've got to model this attitude yourself — which means, no groaning, moping or panicking if you don't win a local business award, don't get a grant, don't win a golf game, don't earn back a client's business, etc. No punishing yourself for making a mistake, either. If your child sees you being hard on yourself ("I'm so stupid! Ugh, how could I mess this up?") then that is the attitude that he or she is likely to mimic, too.

When it comes to overachieving, as well as every other issue described in this book, your job is to model the kind of behavior, values and attitude that you wish to see in your child.

It all starts with you.

Closing words: Abby's new chapter.

Through working with Abby's parents, I learned that ever since Abby was very little, her mother hovered over her, checking in on her, making sure she did everything "perfectly." (Her mother didn't mean to do this, and often wasn't even aware she was doing it.)

Through working with me, Abby's mom realized she had adopted this parenting approach to spare Abby the painful feelings she (mom) had felt growing up in the shadow of her very talented older sibling.

The reality is that Abby's mom never felt that she was "good enough," especially in the shadow of her golden sister.

To spare Abby from feeling that same sense of inadequacy, her mom subconsciously fostered in her a drive to be "the best" — and this made Abby feel compelled to overachieve in order to make her mom happy and feel like she's worth something.

Once Abby's mom realized this, she had some healing conversations with her own inner child. She released the pain she had felt in the past. Then, she sat down with Abby, apologized for holding her to perfectionistic standards, and began the healing process.

This relieved Abby from a lot of self-imposed pressure. She continues to do very well in whatever she does. The difference now is that Abby reaches for the stars because she <u>wants</u> to, not because she feels she <u>has</u> to.

CHAPTER FIVE

*"My child makes such bad decisions!
Terrible time management. Procrastination.
Why can't she get it together?"*

"Heather, it's homework time," says her mother. "And Jake, you know you need to take out the garbage."

"I don't want to do homework now, I'm in the middle of a video game…" says Heather, age eleven. Jake, fourteen, chimes in, "I have lots of time. I'll take the garbage out later."

Heather and Jake's parents came to see me because they're at their wit's end with these children.

"Heather drags her feet with her homework," says her dad. "And Jake postpones doing things because he doesn't see any urgency. He's always saying, 'I'll do it later.' I'm tired of telling him to get organized because he is always running late!"

"I feel so bad for yelling at her recently," says Heather's mom. "But her room was so messy that I couldn't see the floor. Clothes, books and games everywhere! Honestly, I'm so fed up with reminding her to shape up because she can't find what she needs for her homework, forgets her books at school, or leaves her clothes on the floor!"

"By now you've probably realized that nagging and yelling doesn't work," I say to these parents.

They nod emphatically — they're both tired of being the "nag police."

I explain that there are other ways, healthier ways, to bring order back into their children's lives. I also explain that they need to help their children nip their stalling tactics in the bud before a full-blown procrastination habit develops — one that's likely to follow them into adulthood.

Why do children get disorganized, mismanage their time and procrastinate?

In my experience, when children make poor decisions, have poor time management habits and procrastinate, they're emulating — dun dun dun, no surprise here! — their primary role models. Aka: you.

Often, when this situation arises, one or both parents don't have sound time management habits, themselves, and order is not part of their own lives.

It's pretty tough to teach a lesson that you, yourself, have not yet mastered.

Children will see right through your "rules" and think to themselves, "But that's not what you do! So why should I?"

For example: Heather's mom was upset because her daughter's room was so incredibly messy. Yet, through our conversation, I learned that Mom wasn't being fair by requiring Heather to be organized. Heather's mom couldn't even get her car into the garage because it was so jammed with clutter!

At that point, we knew this mom needed to lead by example or Heather wouldn't have any reason to respect her and cooperate.

The next morning, after driving Heather to school, her mom reflected on the state of her car — the seats were covered with papers and magazines, and candy wrappers were all over the floor. "It's a mess," she thought, feeling bad about the impression this made on Heather. That afternoon, she tidied her car and the garage and then told her daughter, "From now on, I'll keep my car and the garage neat and I expect you to do the same with your room."

"But c'mon, she's just a kid!"

It can be tempting to just say, "Well, of course she's disorganized" or "of course he's bad at managing his time" because "After all, s/he's just a kid!"
But that kind of attitude isn't helpful.
Children are adults-in-training, and the sooner that you can instill good time management and organizational skills, the better.
This doesn't mean you are going to hold your seven-year-old to the exact same set of organizational standards to which you might hold your forty-year-old colleague at work — you're going to set age-appropriate expectations, of course. (Refer back to Chapter One of this book for an overview of children's emotional maturity levels, and the types of rules and consequences that can reasonably be applied from ages 0 to 13 and up.)

Self-reflection.

Got a disorganized child on your hands who is struggling with time management?
Here are a few questions to help you see how your upbringing, your past, and your personal choices might have contributed to creating this situation...

- Am I a good role model? (Or do I tell my child to do certain things, but I don't hold myself to the same standard?)
- How are my own time management skills?
- Am I disorganized? Messy?
- Do I procrastinate? Does my child see me procrastinating?
- What kinds of role models did I have while I was growing up? Were my role models disorganized? Neat? Overly fastidious (to the point where I might be choosing to be messy, as an act of defiance or rebellion?)
- Wherever your current behavior stems from, you can create positive changes.

You can start by saying to yourself:

> *"I am no longer a child emulating or reacting to my role models. I am an adult and I can rewrite the script that I still follow — a carryover from my past. I can set a better example for my own child. And I will.*
>
> *It is important to me to be [insert the desired behavior here: neat, organized, punctual, efficient, reliable, etc.] _____ because _____.*
> *That's what I will model for my own child beginning <u>today</u>."*

Once you've had this conversation with yourself, you'll be better equipped to start making some adjustments to your parenting approach — and you'll be more likely to see good results.

On that note, let's discuss solutions to a few common dilemmas:

1. *Goofing off before homework gets finished.*

Like many children, Heather procrastinates on her homework because she hasn't learned to prioritize.

Her parents need to set rules and explain that if she doesn't comply, there will be a consequence ("No video games until your homework and chores are done. If you don't cooperate, you won't be allowed to play video games for one day.")

With this type of rule in place, Heather is likely to be more productive. Children tend to follow rules when they know that if they don't, they'll incur a consequence.

2. *Putting off chores until "later."*

Jake postpones doing his chores because he doesn't see any urgency ("I'll do it later").

Jake's parents need to emphasize that if he doesn't do what's expected, he'll get a consequence ("You are responsible for taking out the garbage immediately after dinner; otherwise no TV that night").

This approach typically motivates children to behave responsibly.

3. *Not starting at all (because of fear).*

Some children put off doing schoolwork and other tasks because they're dealing with low self-esteem ("I'm afraid I'll mess up, so I'm not going to even try").

One way that parents can address this is by reassuring their children, "Your best is good enough. Just try." This can help children who have "perfectionistic" tendencies to begin to relax so they can get started.

4. *Not starting because the task is too daunting.*

Other children drag their feet because a task feels daunting and overwhelming ("I have so much homework, I don't know where to start.").

These children need to be encouraged to break down homework into small tasks by focusing on one assignment at a time, and estimating how long each assignment might take.

Then, instead of staring at a blank page because they're stuck, they can plan a realistic schedule and get their homework done.

A universal solution for all types of time-management and organizational issues:

Use a chart.

If you're reading the chapters in this book in sequential order, starting with Chapter One, you've already heard me tout the benefits of creating a "daily chart" system a few times.

I can't emphasize this enough:

Visual charts can prevent needless drama and arguing, help the whole family stay organized, and turn chaos into order. Charts can be life-changers!

By creating a daily chart that lays out rules, chores, and behavioral expectations — along with consequences for non-compliance — you are helping your child to develop important organizational skills that can set your child up for greater success in the future.

Items on the chart could include: packing their backpack at night for the next school day, wake-up time, mealtimes, designated study time, specified television and electronics time (e.g., using the iPad to post on Instagram), brushing teeth, and bedtime.

(Turn to pages 158-165 of this book for a sample chart that you can use as a template to fill out, along with a few more instructions on how to use charts effectively).

As each task is completed, children can place a checkmark on the chart next to that task. Checking off items gives them a sense of accomplishment ("I finished my homework!"). This can build self-confidence and self-esteem.

Closing words: Order, at last!

During the sessions that I had with Heather and Jake's parents, I was pleased to see them making a concerted effort to set a good example for their children by providing them with a structured home environment.

This included setting up rules and consequences as they taught their children how to prioritize and be more productive and responsible.

It took a while for these parents to be consistent with implementing consequences — which meant that they didn't see consistent compliance from their children right away.

Heather's mom felt bad about implementing consequences. "I feel like I'm being mean," she told me.

I helped her work through those feelings, so she could see that there's nothing "mean" about implementing a consequence. She realized that Heather and Jake have a choice about whether they want to incur a consequence. If they choose to behave in a way that incurs the consequence, then when she implements it, she's not being unfair or cruel — she's being a responsible parent.

To assume your responsibility as a parent and equip your child with life skills, instead of letting them do "whatever they want" as children, only to later find out (in adulthood) that that's not how life works — that's not "mean." That's love.

Heather and Jake's parents also found it useful to create a master calendar outlining dates of family events and school tests, as well as due dates for projects. They posted the calendar on the refrigerator, a central location where their children couldn't miss it.

These days, Heather and Jake are much better able to plan, focus and get things done. Their household is much more peaceful because there's no more nagging and yelling.

Another bonus? The children's self-confidence and sense of independence has gotten a boost as they've both realized that they are capable of being organized and staying on course — which leads to success!

CHAPTER SIX

*"My child has terrible manners!
She's so rude and inconsiderate."*

"My daughter, Sophia, has become so incredibly rude. I don't understand where this behavior is coming from."

Sophia's mom is totally frustrated. This is our first conversation about her fourteen-year-old daughter, so I encourage her to elaborate.

"The other day, her aunt and uncle came over to visit, and when she came home from school she just marched right into her room without even saying 'hello' to them. I practically had to pry her out of her room when it was time for dinner. And then she sulked the entire time, didn't join the conversation, and barely touched her food."

Sophia's mom sighs heavily.

"And here's the worst part: when I asked her why she wasn't eating, she declared that she's vegan now, and that people who eat meat are 'disgusting murderers'. Can you believe that? She said that right at the dinner table! I was so stunned, I literally didn't know what to say. I just gaped at her."

Sophia's mom goes on to tell me that her daughter is a bright, talented girl, but her behavior is becoming increasingly worrisome.

She's worried that her daughter's rudeness is going to land her in big trouble in the future — especially if she starts to sass-talk her teachers or, in the not-too-distant future, if she's rude to her employers when she's old enough to get a summer job.

Sophia's mom affirms, repeatedly, that she has "no idea" where her daughter's defiant behavior is coming from.

Clearly, we've got a bit of digging to do to identify the source of this issue.

Why do "good children" become "rude little monsters"?

First off, a reminder:

Children are not born rude, insolent or inconsiderate. "Rudeness" is learned behavior. (Which, fortunately, means that it can be unlearned, too.)

In my experience, when children are rude, the source of the issue can usually be traced back to one of three things:

1. Poor role models.

If children are defiant and rude, it could be because they are mimicking what they have seen in their own household, on TV, in the media, and possibly at their friends' homes.

It is your responsibility, as a parent, to closely monitor your child's media exposure, and to chat with the parents of your child's friends, to see how these friends are being raised, what values their parents have, and whether these values coincide with your own.

2. Overly lenient parenting.

Some parents want to protect their children from experiencing pain, frustration, or failure of any kind, so — despite their best intentions — they wind up coddling their children, giving them "whatever they want, whenever they want."

This parenting approach often stems from a parent's own childhood. If you were raised in a home where you felt ignored, for example, you might feel driven to make sure your own children never feel that way. You might over-compensate and wind up raising children who are used to being catered to like royalty and hearing "yes" to every request.

3. *Overly strict parenting.*

If you have perfectionistic tendencies, hold your child to unfairly high standards, or set severe consequences for minor infractions, your child may eventually "rebel" against your strict parenting style by swinging to the other end of the spectrum — becoming crude, rude, vulgar, and defiant, as a means of differentiating from you.

Regardless of the source of the issue, "rude children" are ultimately dealing with the same situation: they need to "grow up" emotionally. The child might be eight, ten or fifteen years old, but their "emotional age" is stuck back in the infant / toddler zone (you know, when it's all about "instant gratification"). They're stuck in a level of emotional immaturity that goes like this:

"I want what I want when I want it! And if I don't get it, I'll have a tantrum until I do! And if that means being rude and hurtful to my parents or anyone else who is in my way, then so be it!"

Self-reflection.

Got a rude child on your hands?

- Here are a few questions to help you see how your upbringing, your past, and your personal choices might have contributed to creating this situation…
- Where did my child learn to behave this way? (Is he or she emulating me, my partner, a friend's parents, a character on TV, etc.?)
- Do I supervise and monitor my child's experiences to make sure that they're being exposed to role models who are polite, courteous and considerate?
- Do I model polite, considerate behavior for my children?
- Have I been so focused on my child's wellbeing that they have learned to only be concerned about themselves and no one else?

- Have I clearly explained to my child that rude behavior is unacceptable, and why?
- Have I clearly outlined for my child what kind of behavior is acceptable and not acceptable?
- Have I clearly laid out for my child what the consequence for rude behavior will be?
- Have I had my child repeat back to me what rude behavior is, why it is not acceptable, and what the consequence for rude behavior will be — so that I can make sure that my child understands the rules?
- Have I instructed anyone that I entrust to supervise or care for my child (including grandparents, babysitters, etc.) about my stance on rude behavior? Do they know that I need to be notified if my child is engaging in rude behavior so that I can impose the appropriate consequence?

Finding solutions.

Children behave rudely because somewhere, somehow, they have picked up that this kind of behavior is "OK" — meaning, they have seen others do it — and they have been allowed to get away with it.

Sometimes, especially when children are young and behave inappropriately, they actually get attention for it. Their parents think it is cute and funny. These children form a connection: "If I behave rudely, then mom and dad will smile and laugh!" So then the children keep doing it, because we all like getting attention from people we look up to!

The solution is to lay down firm rules about what kind of behavior is acceptable and what is not, and then, of course, to implement those rules consistently.

Start by having a private conversation (no children within earshot) with your spouse or co-parent, if you have one.

Together, you need to agree that...

- As parents, we need to model politeness, courtesy and respect.

- We need to pay close attention to our children and monitor and supervise their behavior.
- We need to always know where our children are, who they are with, and what they are doing.
- We need to have conversations with other caregivers, babysitters, and influential figures to make sure that our children are being exposed to the right kinds of role models (and that our rules are being implemented even when we are not present).
- We need to stop catering to our children and giving into their whims. (If this is the case.)

Once both of you have discussed and agreed to the basic terms, then it's time to get the children involved. You can do this by holding a "family meeting."

Start the meeting by taking responsibility for the role that you have played in creating this situation. This models "personal responsibility" and "self awareness" for your child, which is very valuable for them to witness.

Here's a script you can use (feel free to adapt it to suit your scenario, of course):

"We're sorry that we haven't been better parents to you.

We have really let your behavior get out of hand. That is going to change.

It is our responsibility to teach you how to behave in a polite, respectful way.

If you continue to behave disrespectfully, like when [describe a recent incident], there could be serious consequences. (For example, you could get expelled from school;) and if you behave like this as an adult, there could be serious consequences as well. (For example, no one will want to hire you for a job.) We can't, in good conscience, support that.

From now on this is what we expect: Respectful answers, polite responses, eye contact, alert posture (no slouching or acting like you're doing us a favor by talking to us or responding to something that we say), showing appreciation, being helpful around the house (and not only when we ask... but taking initiative as well), [list any other expectations you have].

It is a privilege to live in this house. It is a privilege to be part of this family. You need to start showing appreciation.

You have many privileges, like electronics, playdates, sleepovers, your favorite foods and desserts, etc. You will lose those privileges if you don't behave considerately. Do you understand?"

Have your child verbally repeat everything back to you so that you are 100% sure they understand.

Then, as I've suggested in previous chapters, create a chart that outlines the specific behaviors you wish to see and the consequences for non-compliance.

Monitor your child's behavior closely and start doing a daily "chart check" to see how things are progressing. If your chart checking is consistent — and you are consistent with applying consequences as needed — you are likely to see a positive shift.

Closing words: Sophia's turnaround.

Sophia's mom and I continued to work together for several weeks, both in person and over the phone, and sometimes virtually via Internet video calls.

She held a family meeting with her daughter and was surprised to discover that it went better than expected.

Sophia's mom took a wise approach. Given her daughter's recent interest in animal rights and vegan preferences, she posed the question, "Wouldn't you agree that it's important to treat animals with respect and care?" Her daughter emphatically agreed. Then Sophia's mom asked, "Well, what about human beings? We're animals, too. Do you feel that humans deserve respect, too?" Her daughter hadn't thought about it that way before, but she agreed that her mom had a point.

This opened up a beautiful dialogue about why it's important to treat people with politeness and consideration. Sophia's mom told me that, in the past, she's never really given her daughter a good "reason" to behave politely — she just told her to "do it." This conversation helped her daughter to understand the reasoning behind the rules.

Following my recommendations, they created a chart that they pinned to the bulletin board in the kitchen outlining acceptable behavior and consequences for choosing not to comply. There were a few slip ups at first, but Sophia eventually got on board — especially after losing her cell phone privileges for an entire weekend. (Something she did <u>not</u> want to experience again!).

At a later follow up session, Sophia's mom reported that her daughter's behavior had gone through a major turnaround.

"The other day, I found her in the kitchen writing a beautiful, polite 'thank you' note to one of her relatives who had given her a birthday gift. I didn't have to ask her to do it or remind her to do it. She did it all on her own."

CHAPTER SEVEN

"My child is shy and has a hard time making friends."

Olivia's mom and dad are sitting in my office because they received a troubling phone call from their daughter's preschool director.

"Our daughter is four and recently started preschool," Olivia's dad explains. "She's very shy and the preschool director says that she sits alone at playtime and she's not making friends."

"At home, Olivia plays with her siblings and cousins," says Mom. "But she doesn't try to make friends with other kids in the neighborhood."

They go on to explain that Olivia keeps her distance from people she doesn't know. She often clings to her parents' legs or wants to sit on their lap instead of socializing.

They are not sure if this kind of behavior is "OK" or if they have something to worry about.

Olivia's dad shares with me that he's always been "introverted" and isn't particularly chatty or social. He wonders if his daughter has absorbed some of his traits and tendencies.

Why are some children so shy?

Some children are innately more extroverted and outgoing than others. That's natural.

But when a child becomes so "shy" that he or she struggles to make friends, struggles to speak up in school, or struggles to even make eye contact, that's not a good thing.

Why does this happen? There are several frequently occurring causes.

In some instances, the child has been overprotected. Perhaps the child hasn't been introduced to many people outside of the family, nor been taught how to communicate with people he or she doesn't know.

In other instances, the child might be emulating one or both parents. Perhaps mom is quite shy around strangers herself, or dad prefers to read alone rather than join the family for dinner.

In other instances, the child might be dealing with feelings of "shame" and low self-esteem. Perhaps, as a very small child, a parent barked, "Shame on you! NO!" after the child spilled some juice or accidentally dropped something which made a loud noise. Perhaps a grandparent harshly reprimanded the child, "Don't speak unless you are spoken to." These kinds of "scolding" incidents, while relatively minor in the grand scheme of things, can still leave emotional bruises that impact the child's behavior in the future.

Self-reflection.

Got a shy child who is having difficulty coming out of his or her shell?

Here are a few questions that can be helpful to see how your upbringing, your past, and your personal choices might have contributed to creating this situation…

- Do you consider yourself to be a shy person?
- How do you behave around strangers, people in the neighborhood, new friends, etc.?
- Does your child see you engaged in conversations with people around the neighborhood? Or are you usually "checked out," staring at your phone while talking, aloof or disengaged?

- Do you have feelings of fear or insecurity when you're in social settings, like parties or work functions where you don't know very many people? Do you avoid those situations all together? Does your child overhear you complaining about how much you'd rather just stay home and not go?
- Do you think you may have unknowingly / inadvertently harshly scolded your child for "speaking up" or being "noisy" or too "chatty" in the past?
- Who are the primary caregivers / role models in your child's life? Are these people friendly and communicative? Or shy and withdrawn?

Finding solutions.

If your child is very shy, one powerful course of action for you, as the parent, would be to set a healthy example. Give your child a good role model to follow.

Examples of good role modeling include…

- Showing your child how to say "hello" to potential playmates. Encourage your child to follow your example. You say, "Hello, David, nice to meet you." David replies, "Hello, nice to meet you, too." To which you say, "Olivia, can you say hello to David, too?" If your child shies away or refuses to speak, use this moment as an opportunity for some "re-training. Tell your child, "When one of your classmates says hello, you say hello back. It's safe and it's OK to do that."
- Engaging in friendly conversations throughout the day — chatting with the mail deliverer, bus driver, grocery store clerk, and so on. Let your child see you smiling, making eye contact, listening, and engaging. This will model healthy communication for your child.
- Talking excitedly about fun experiences with friends and then inviting your child to talk about his or her own friends. "I had such a great walk with Sandra! I am so grateful to

have such great friends. Who are your friends right now? What do you like about them?"

Closing words: Coming out of her shell.

Olivia's parents reported "slow progress" with their four-year-old daughter initially.

They tried to set up a couple of playdates with new children from around the neighborhood, but Olivia hovered around her mom and hid behind her legs much of the time.

Slowly but surely, though, Olivia began to come out of her shell.

Her mother reported back to me that Olivia seemed to respond particularly positively when her mom "took the lead."

"I would squat on the ground, at eye level with Olivia's new playmate, and say 'hello'. Then I'd start playing a game with her new playmate. Olivia would see us having a good time, smiling and laughing, and eventually, she'd come over and get involved in the game. Pretty soon she'd be totally engaged, I'd step away and she'd continue playing with her new friend."

Lately, Olivia has been playing and talking to other children without her mom always needing to get the ball rolling. A huge improvement!

Olivia's father has been making an effort to come out of his own shell a bit more, too — joining in at family barbecues and social gatherings and trying to set a good example for his daughter.

"I don't want to 'force' her to be a 'social butterfly' if that's not her true personality," her father tells me at a follow up visit. "But I recognize now that her shyness could have become a bigger problem later down the line. I'm glad we intervened early and it's been good for me to take a closer look at my own behavior, too."

CHAPTER EIGHT

"My child is overweight."

Lori's daughter Sarah, age ten, needs to lose weight.

Sarah's classmates tease her about her size, which brings her to tears.

Lori has a history of dropping unwanted pounds through quick-fix diets and then putting them back on, plus more.

I've been working with Lori on her overeating and now that she is well on her way to achieving her weight goals, she's ready to tackle Sarah's weight issue, too.

"Sarah hasn't always been fat like this. How do I bring this up to her without hurting her feelings?" Lori asks me. "I don't want her to feel worse than she already does."

I suggest that Lori take Sarah to the doctor for a check-up:

"The doctor will probably mention that she's over the ideal weight-range for a girl of her age, at her height. After the appointment, you could follow up by saying, *'I'd like to talk about what we can do to help you drop some pounds.'* You could then explain to Sarah that she's eating more than her body needs, and suggest she change her eating habits by, for example, limiting junk food and adding exercise into her day."

I encourage Lori to talk to Sarah in an age-appropriate way:

"She may not grasp the connection between being overweight and future health threats like heart problems," I explained. "But she'll understand the idea that, 'If you add fruits and veggies to your diet and play outside more, you'll be able to swim without getting tired.' You could also point out that a healthy lifestyle could improve her looks ('Your hair will be shinier if you eat better') and offer an incentive ('As you trim down, we'll be able to shop for new clothes')."

I also emphasize to Lori that if she wants Sarah to be healthier, she <u>must</u> continue to set a good example for her daughter:

"Modeling a healthy lifestyle is just as important as modeling qualities like integrity and thoughtfulness," I explain. "When Sarah sees you prioritizing good eating habits and exercise, she'll want to eat better and be more active, too, just like her mommy."

None of the children (or adults) that I have coached over the past 29 years were born overweight, or with a desire to eat more food than their bodies require. This was learned behavior, which meant (happily) that it could be unlearned, too.

Self-reflection.

Is your child overeating and struggling with his or her weight?
Here are a few questions to help you see how your upbringing, your past, and your personal choices might have contributed to creating this situation…

- Do I eat for emotional reasons? (When I feel lonely, angry, or bored, do I turn to food for comfort?)
- As a child, did I and / or my parents eat for emotional reasons?
- Do I reward myself with food?
- As a child, was I rewarded with food? (For example: "Do your chores and you can have a brownie.")

- If I have a slip up (i.e., overeat) do I try to remedy this with a fad diet?
- Has my child overheard me saying things like, "Oh, sure, I'll take another slice — I can always start my diet on Monday!" and other statements that make the binge-diet-binge-diet pattern seem "OK"?
- Do I cycle between weight loss and weight gain?
- Do I model healthy eating habits for my children?
- Do I have plenty of passions outside of food? Or is food THE most exciting thing in my entire life?

Finding solutions.

The best way to teach your child about the importance of healthy eating and exercise is to model those behaviors yourself.

If you're struggling with your own weight, first, focus on improving your own habits.

Then, once you're making strides in the right direction, you will probably be in a position where you can model good habits and set new ground rules for your children without being deemed a "hypocrite."

Here are a few approaches to try:

- *Model healthy "emotional management."*

This is a big one.

If you don't know how to manage your emotions without turning to food for comfort, then that's a pattern your child will be likely to emulate, too.

So, if you overeat regularly, try to identify what kinds of emotions are driving you to do this.

Are you sad? Bored? Annoyed? Craving company? Entertainment? Ask yourself: "What's really bothering me? What am I really hungry for?" Although emotional eating can offer relief from stressful emotions, this reprieve is only temporary.

- *Help your child to become more aware of his or her emotions, too.*

If you see your child poking around in the fridge just after a snack or mealtime, for example, you can ask, "Sweetheart, are you really hungry right now? What are you feeling right now? Let's talk about it." Open up a conversation and invite your child to answer honestly. Listen without judgment.

Based on what your child says, you can recommend a healthier solution. ("It sounds like you're feeling lonely. How about we get on Skype and talk to Grandma? Or play a game together?").

- *STOP the crash dieting.*

If you have a pattern of overeating, then going on a crash diet, losing weight, then regaining it all, plus more, I urge you: <u>stop the pattern now</u>.

Research has shown that when it comes to permanent weight loss, dieting does not work. What does work is learning to eat for physical reasons (to fuel your body) not for emotional reasons (to soothe loneliness, stress, boredom, etc.), along with committing to a balanced lifestyle: eating wholesome, nutritious foods, indulging in treats on occasion, and moving your body often.

- *Use charts to outline and reinforce good habits.*

Try using a chart system to track meal plans and fitness goals.

Encourage your child to add checkmarks or gold stars to the daily chart when he or she makes good choices, like choosing a healthy snack (fresh fruit instead of a candy bar) or choosing an outdoor activity (like bicycling around the block instead of playing video games).

With each checkmark, your child's self-esteem gets a boost!

- *Remind your child that there are lots of things to get excited about and look forward to — other than food.*

Show your child that the world is full of beautiful experiences, pleasures, and things to get excited about, and they don't involve food.

Definitely avoid using food as a "reward" for commendable behavior.

If your child goes "above and beyond" — like receiving a "Most Improved" award from the school's gym instructor — you can praise your child and offer a non-food reward, like a new t-shirt or a comic book that he or she's been wanting.

Closing words: Making progress, together.

Lori followed my advice and took her daughter, Sarah, to the doctor for a check up.

They had a conversation afterwards and Sarah seemed receptive to making some changes in order to slim down and reach a healthier weight.

The next day, they went grocery shopping together and picked out healthy foods.

Lori and Sarah both committed to spending less time watching TV and instant-messaging with friends on the computer, and more time doing physical activities.

They began walking before dinner on weeknights and worked out together on the weekends, using an exercise DVD.

Lori continued to pursue her own health and weight loss goals, diving deeply into self-awareness to identify why she'd gotten herself into a habit of overeating.

She began to realize that her nighttime bingeing typically stemmed from a place of anger and loneliness within herself. Her husband worked night shifts, leaving her home alone, and she often felt resentful and abandoned, turning to food for comfort.

This realization was huge for Lori.

Equipped with this self-awareness, she was able to "check in" with herself before walking towards the fridge when she wasn't physically hungry. She began journaling her feelings and finding other ways to manage pent-up emotions without turning to food.

When Lori checked in with me again, several weeks later, she was pleased to report that she was doing much better and that she and Sarah were both losing weight.

"I still love food and I look forward to meals," she told me. "But I don't reward myself, or Sarah, with food anymore. And when I'm angry or stressed, I turn to food less and less."

Lori also expressed how much she enjoyed her evening walk with Sarah. It gave them a chance to talk, connect, and enjoy quality time together.

"I used to dread exercise," she confessed. "But now I am realizing that it doesn't have to be torturous. My evening walk with Sarah has become one of the best parts of my day."

CHAPTER NINE

*"My child is dating and might be having sex.
I'm so worried."*

Kennedy's parents are distraught. Kennedy, age fifteen, has been lying to them about her whereabouts after school. On a recent occasion, she said she was going to study at a friend's house, but secretly, she went on a date instead.

Kennedy's parents found out about it and now they are wondering, "What <u>else</u> has she lied to us about?" They worry that their daughter might already be having sex, or engaging in other risky behaviors, but they're not sure and Kennedy refuses to talk about it.

"She's too young for this," her dad tells me. "We didn't raise her to behave this way. We don't know if she's getting pressure from her peers at school to start dating, or what, but this has got to stop."

"But what can we do?" her mom asks. She says they've already tried talking to Kennedy about why it's so important to be protective of her body, and why it's a good idea to wait until she's older to have sex, but she just rolls her eyes and tunes them out.

They're terrified she'll get pregnant, get a sexually transmitted disease, or worse.

I listen and my heart breaks for these parents.

The frustrating reality is that, by age fifteen, Kennedy's beliefs about sex, intimacy, dating, and self-respect have already been pretty firmly cemented. In just a few years, she'll legally be an adult, probably away at college or no longer living at home. It's going to be tough for her parents to change her beliefs and behavior at this point.

But is it a hopeless situation? Absolutely not.

There is <u>always</u> a way to try to steer your child out of harm's way.

And as a parent, it is not optional that you try to do so. It's a must.

Why does this situation happen?

When children are engaging in risky sexual behavior, like sexting, chatting with strangers online, or dating without permission, there may be several issues at play.

For starters…

- As a parent, you may have not taught your child important lessons about "self-respect" during the early, formative years.

Maybe your child witnessed you treating your body without much care and respect.

Maybe your child overheard you bragging about wild sexual conquests from "back in your college days."

Or maybe your child witnessed an ever-rotating cast of new boyfriends or girlfriends going in and out of your bedroom.

Remember: as your child's primary role model, you set the tone for what's acceptable and what's not.

- You may have (unknowingly) "shamed" your child for engaging in natural sexual exploration (for example, by yelling angrily, "Don't touch yourself there!" at a toddler who has no idea that it is inappropriate to touch "down there" when in public). As a result, your now-older child may feel like he or she has to "sneak around" when it comes to sex and sexual curiosity, hiding things from you, rather than risk getting caught.

- It's also possible that you and your partner, spouse or co-parent are not on the same page when it comes to sex and dating. Maybe you think that dating is fine, but your partner does not agree. If your rules on dating are flimsy, inconsistent, or non-existent, or if your child sees the two of you disagreeing about what's OK, then your child may play one of you against the other, hoping that whoever is more lenient will side with him or her "so I can have my way!"
- Of course, it's also possible that your child has been exposed to poor role models (including characters in the media and on TV) who engage in risky sexual behavior, without incurring a consequence. Perhaps you didn't monitor your child's media exposure closely enough in the past. But all of that can change now.

Self-reflection.

Worried about your child's choices and attitudes towards dating and sex?

Here are a few questions to help you see how your upbringing, your past, and your personal choices might have contributed to creating this situation…

- Did I put off having "the talk" about sex with my child? If so, why did I put it off? (Was I ashamed, uncomfortable, just didn't know what to say, etc.?)
- How do I feel about talking to my child about sex and dating now? OK? Uncomfortable?
- How do I feel about setting new rules (like a nightly curfew) for my children now? OK? Uncomfortable?
- Does my partner / spouse / co-parent have the same stance that I do? Are we on the same page?
- Am I modeling self-respect through my words and actions? Am I setting a good example for what a healthy, self-respecting, loving relationship can look like?

Finding solutions.

If your child is engaging in risky sexual behavior, my suggestion is to hold a family meeting as soon as possible.

You could begin by apologizing to your child for allowing this situation to develop. Take responsibility for the role that you played. This shows your child that you're not here to scold or shame them. It also reinforces that you are the adult in charge.

You might try saying:

"We need to have a conversation about dating and sex. This may sound strange coming from me, since I have not really discussed these topics with you before — and I want to apologize to you for that.

As your parent, it's my responsibility to teach you all about dating and sex, about when, how and with whom. I should have had this talk with you a long time ago, but I did not do that, and I'm sorry for that. But that changes now."

Share with your child that you want them to enjoy loving, beautiful relationships in the future.

Explain that you understand how exciting it can be to have a crush on someone, develop strong feelings for someone, or even fall in love.

Explain, too, that sometimes these emotions can prompt us to make risky, unhealthy choices — choices with serious consequences, like pregnancy or contracting incurable diseases.

Share with your child that — just like there are rules that protect you while you're on the road driving a car — there are going to be some firm rules for dating, too.

"We're going to have some new rules about dating from this day forward. These rules are to ensure your safety. These rules are not optional and there will be consequences if you choose not to comply."

Outline the rules that you've chosen along with your partner and the consequences for violating each rule.

Have your child repeat back the new rules to you, so you know he or she understands.

If your child complains or insists that these rules are unnecessary, hold firm. Say:

"I wish that were true, but as your parent, it is my responsibility to keep you safe and give you every possible chance at a happy, successful future.

These rules are for your safety and wellbeing.

If you prove to me that you can comply with these rules — and show me, through your actions, that you can be trusted — then later down the line, we can talk about adjusting the rules to give you more independence. But for now, the rules we've just talked about are not optional."

Holding a family meeting to go over the new rules is great — but "talking" to your child is not enough.

"Conversations" can be a good starting point, but conversations alone rarely influence children's decisions, especially when curiosity, peer pressure and raging hormones are involved!

What <u>does</u> influence children's decisions?

Supervision, rules, and consequences.

On that note, here are three of the most powerful things that you can do to keep your child safe:

1. Supervise dates.

Know where your children are, who they are with and what they are doing, at all times. This means supervising your teenager's dates.

"Supervised dating" may seem like a relic from the 1950's, but it's up to you as a parent to ensure that your teen's dates are safe. Supervision is THE best way to do that. Sometimes, it's the ONLY way.

So, what does a supervised date look like? It could mean...

- Allowing your older teen daughter to spend time alone in her bedroom with her boyfriend, to give them some privacy, but keeping the door propped open the whole time.
- Taking your teenage son, his date and a group of friends to the mall and reading a book at a nearby table, while they have lunch, hold hands and chat.
- Escorting your teen to the movies, with a date, and then sitting in the back row while they sit in the middle section — to give them a little space, but not total seclusion.

The message should be clear: "Make good choices. I'm right here."

Use your own judgment to decide how much supervision is necessary, but always err on the side of caution. All it takes is one slip-up to lead to an unplanned pregnancy, or some other consequence that could derail your child's entire life.

2. *Monitor online activity.*

To keep your teen safe, online, remember these 4 words:

Supervise. Review. Educate. Block.

Supervise online activity with a tracking app, and situate the computer that your teen uses at home in a visible area, like the living room. Nearly 30% of teens have been contacted by a total stranger online. Supervision is crucial!

Review your teenager's social media profiles (Facebook, Twitter, Instagram, Pinterest). Often. If you see something troubling, like scantily clad photos of your teenage daughter at a college party, set new rules — and consequences — right away.

Educate your teen about the dangers of posting sensitive information online — like your address, phone number or last name. Emphasize that information that's posted online is trackable, forever — even if you delete it. (Tools like the Wayback Machine mean that even deleted info can be recovered by people who really want to find it.)

Block certain sites (like porn sites, adult chat rooms and online dating sites) so that your teen cannot access them, period. SafeGuard is a popular site-blocking tool. If you're unclear about how to block sites, find a friendly computer pro who can help.

3. *Enforce consequences <u>consistently</u>.*

It's not uncommon for teens to throw caution to the wind and test the limits. They're at that age where they think they know everything, that they're invincible, and that adults are, well... "old-fashioned."

It's up to you to teach them that risky actions can have serious consequences. You can help teach this valuable life lesson by enforcing consequences of your own at home.

Be sure to let your teen know, in advance, what the rules are (for example: "you have a 9pm curfew on Friday night.")

Be sure to let your teen know, at that time, what the consequences will be if a rule is violated (for example: "if you violate the 9pm curfew, you will be grounded for two weeks.")

Be sure to implement reasonable consequences consistently, or your teen will not take you seriously and you'll be faced with one violation after another.

The purpose of these consequences is not to make your teen's life miserable. In fact, ideally, the consequence would never have to be enforced! Its purpose is to discourage poor choices ("I don't want to be grounded, so I'll be home by my 9pm curfew.") Make sure that the consequence is distasteful enough so that it gets your teen's attention, prompting your son or daughter to make a wise choice.

One day, thanks to your firm, loving parenting, your teen will be all grown-up — capable of making smart, self-respecting decisions without your supervision and guidance.

But until that day, it's up to you to keep your teenager safe.

Your teen might not like it. Your teen might not like <u>you</u>, at least right now.

But one day, your teen will be grateful.

Because you've given him or her the greatest gift and privilege of all:

A chance at a happy future, unburdened by consequences that could have easily been prevented.

Closing words: It's never too late to influence your teen.

Kennedy was not happy about the changes that her parents chose to make — particularly the part about "supervised dates."

She complained bitterly and insisted that this idea was totally "old-fashioned" and "ridiculous," and none of her friends' parents did this kind of thing.

But her mom and dad held firm, out of deep concern for their daughter. There was one incident where Kennedy tried to sneak around behind their back, but after revoking her cell phone privileges for two weeks, that behavior quickly stopped.

Kennedy's parents are still concerned about what will happen once their young daughter leaves home and goes off to college, but they know that — at least while she is living under their roof — she will be supervised, cared for, and held to certain standards of behavior.

"We know we can't control every single minute of our daughter's life," her father told me at a follow-up session. "And we know that she is going to make her own choices. But we can try to influence her choices as much as possible, and we can take reasonable steps to keep her out of harm's way. That's what we're focusing on. These days, we're feeling empowered instead of just... lost and confused about what to do."

I encourage Kennedy's parents to continue to take advantage of this precious time that they still have together, under one roof, before their daughter leaves home.

She's already a young woman, with her own opinions, but when it comes to instilling important lessons about sex, dating, and relationships, it is never too late to try to make a difference. Even if it feels like your teen isn't responding, keep trying. Show your child that you care enough... not to give up.

CHAPTER TEN

"My child is tech-addicted! I can't get him to unplug from his phone."

Fourteen-year-old Ellie just came home from school. A quiet girl, without many close friends at her new school, she's feeling lonely because she doesn't have a boyfriend.

Ellie logs onto an online dating site and lies about her birthdate so that she can start an account. She uploads a few photos and within minutes, she receives a message:

"Great photo, you're cute. Let's talk or meet, we have lots in common."

Ellie feels a surge of excitement, receiving this attention from a man who claims to be 18 — just a few years older than her. This guy doesn't know that she's not popular at school. Online, she can create a new "persona" and be whoever she wants to be ...

Thirteen-year-old Steven is hooked on gaming and is rarely seen without his iPhone glued to his fingertips. His parents catch him texting and gaming at the dinner table, after bedtime, and he even got in trouble for gaming during one of his classes at school. It's getting out of control.

His parents are baffled. Why can't he just put the %$*# phone down?!

Scenarios like these — and others — are all-too-common.

Whether it's the allure of online dating or computer games, or the quick-burst feeling of "connection" that texting and social media can provide, many children are totally tethered to their devices these days. Sometimes, with dangerous consequences. (At the very least: it's annoying for parents who want to enjoy stimulating conversation with the children they're carpooling to school — without hearing bleeping and dinging every five seconds!)

Just as with dating and sex — which we covered in the previous chapter — having a "conversation" with your child about technology is a good start, but it's not enough.

"Conversations" alone rarely influence children's decisions. Supervision, rules and consequences do.

Self-reflection.

Got a tech-addicted child who is superglued to his or her iPad, phone, computer or tablet?

Here are a few questions to help you see how your upbringing, your past, and your personal choices might have contributed to creating this situation...

- What's my relationship with technology?
- Am I constantly glued to a device, thereby showing my child — through my example — that this kind of behavior is OK?
- Do I feel intimidated by technology? And if so, do I take a hands-off approach with my children? (Like: "I don't know anything about social media, so I can't intervene. I guess I'll just let my child be.")
- Do I rely on technology to make me feel "valuable" or "lovable"? Is my mood dependent on how many re-tweets or Facebook likes I've received that day?
- Do I expose myself inappropriately online? (Oversharing details from my own life or posting revealing, sexual photos, for example, even though I don't want my child to do the same?)

- Where does my relationship with technology come from? (Am I following my parents' example? Do I emulate my partner? My friends?)

Finding solutions.

There are lots of things you can do to help your child develop a healthier, more balanced relationship with technology.
Here are a few basic guidelines…

- *Monitor online activity.*

If you read the previous chapter on dating and sex, you'll probably remember these 4 words:

- *Supervise. Review. Educate. Block.*

Here's a quick review:
Supervise your child's online activity (and phone activity) with a tracking app. Situate the computer that your child uses at home in a visible area, like the living room.
Review your child's social media profiles (Facebook, Twitter, Instagram, Pinterest). Be aware of what your teen is posting and how often.
Educate your child about the dangers of posting sensitive information online — like your address, phone number or last name. Emphasize that information that's posted online is trackable, forever — even if you delete it. (Tools like the Wayback Machine reveal that even deleted info can be recovered by people who really want to find it.)
Block inappropriate and potentially dangerous sites (like porn sites, adult chat rooms and online dating sites) so that your child cannot access them, period. If you're unclear about how to block sites, find a friendly computer pro who can help.

- *Google your child.*

Google your child (and yourself) periodically to see what pops up. You might be shocked!

- *Explain to your child that you are not "anti-technology," just "pro balance."*

You can say,

"I know that the internet is so helpful when it comes to your homework, and I don't know what we'd do without cell phones for staying in touch, and listening to music on an mp3 player is awesome. But you need to know your limits, and to be successful, you can't have electronics ruling your life 24 / 7."

- *Be a good role model.*

Parental role modeling is huge when it comes to technology: review your own social media usage, your own cell phone usage, your own relationship with technology before addressing this issue with your children.

Closing words: Respect tech, strive for balance.

Technology is a double-edged sword. There is so much to learn from it, so much it can teach us, but it can become dangerous if you don't limit your child's access and participation. (Not to mention: your own.)

Strive to be a good role model. Show your child that technology is amazing, but be sure to teach safe practices, then monitor your child closely and enforce the rules you've set.

Create pockets of tech-free time for your family to just "be" together — talking, preparing meals, walking, laughing, working on non-digital projects, enjoying each other's company. (One of my clients banned cell phones at the dinner table and reported that it immediately changed her relationship with her husband and her child.)

In our highly digitalized world, tech-free moments are increasingly rare — and so very precious.

So, as often as possible, turn off all the devices.

Give your child the gift of your undivided attention.

No techie distractions. Just pure love.

CHAPTER ELEVEN

"My child is being bullied and teased at school."

A group of boys at 12-year-old Ashley's new school started teasing her and calling her "fat" and "stupid." She was devastated and didn't want to go to school anymore.

Her parents came to see me because they were upset about the teasing and worried about their daughter's self esteem. But they weren't sure what to do next.

"Should we tell Ashley to ignore these boys and try to avoid them? Should we tell her to go get a teacher if this kind of teasing happens again?" her mother wondered.

"She doesn't want to go to school. Should we tell her she doesn't have a choice? We don't want to be cruel or make her more upset than she already is. But she can't just stay home and skip school!" her dad added.

Both parents hoped that if I spoke to Ashley directly, she might open up a bit more. "She's not telling us any details about the situation at school," her parents explained. "But she might talk to you."

Typically, I work with parents to help them communicate more effectively with their children, rather than intervening on their behalf. But since Ashley was reluctant to talk to her parents, and it was important that she talk to someone, I agreed to meet with her.

Teasing and bullying at school is one of the most stressful situations that a child can endure. Every situation is unique, so every situation ought to be handled differently.

This is definitely a scenario where it's up to you, as the parent, to trust your instincts about how to proceed.

The general guidelines I'm about to share can help you to assess the bullying situation and find solutions without "hovering" too closely or trying to "guard" your child from the difficulties of the world.

The goal is to keep your child safe while empowering him (or her) to successfully navigate all kinds of inter-personal dynamics out in the world.

Finding solutions.

If you suspect — or know for certain — that your child is being teased or bullied, it's important to step in and provide support in a manner that is age-appropriate as well as appropriate to the severity of the situation.

Here are some general guidelines to keep in mind:

- *Don't overreact.*

If your child shares with you that he or she is being bullied (or if you find out some other way) don't overreact.

Let your child speak and listen calmly. Then consider saying to your child, "That sounds like a stressful situation and I'm sorry you had to experience that. I will help you to find a solution to this problem."

Resist the urge to declare something like, "Tomorrow, when I drop you off at school, I'm going to find that boy and give him a piece of my mind!"

- *Don't accuse or be critical.*

Avoid asking questions like, "What did you do to cause this boy to tease you?" That type of question sounds accusatory, as if your child did something "wrong" and "deserves" to be the victim of bullying. Your child needs your support, not finger-pointing or blame.

Reassure your child that the bullying is not his or her fault. She or he did not cause it. Explain that children who bully invariably have personal problems, like feeling powerless or insecure, so they try to make other people feel weak so that they can feel stronger — but deep down, they just want love and approval like everybody else.

- *Ask questions. Stay calm.*

Try asking your child a series of blame-free questions about the situation, like:

"Tell me all about what happened today."
"How did it feel to be spoken to like that?"
"How well do you know this boy / girl?"
"How are his / her grades?"
"Does s / he have many friends?"

Don't interrupt. Let your child talk. Let your child feel the comfort of being seen and heard, without criticism.

If your child says something that makes you feel angry ("That bully is a MONSTER!"), take a deep breath. Stay calm. Do not say something "threatening" about what you'd "like to do…" to the bully — this could cause your child to clam up to avoid upsetting you any further, or because your anger is disturbing or bothersome, or simply because your child is dealing with his / her own emotions and can't deal with your emotions as well.

- *Generate a solution <u>with</u> your child's input.*

You can say something like, "This is a frustrating problem. What is one good solution that you can think of? What do you think we ought to do next?" Coming up with a solution, together, can be an empowering experience for your child.

If your child is unwilling to discuss potential solutions with you, see if s / he might be willing to speak to someone else instead. For example, in my session with 12-year-old Ashley, we decided that if the boys at school called her "fat" or "stupid" again, she would respond by saying, "That's totally uncool." Ashley felt proud of this idea and felt empowered, knowing that she came up with it on her own.

- *Talk to your child's teachers.*

If the bullying that your child is experiencing is happening consistently — not just a one-time occurrence — it may be helpful to meet with your child's teachers or administrators at school.

Make an appointment and explain to the teacher that you wish to keep the conversation confidential. (In other words, you don't want the teacher to stand up in front of the entire class the next day to say, "Ashley's parents came to see me yesterday and we need to have a class discussion about bullying…" and so on). Your child's privacy is important!

Resist the urge to "blame" the teacher for "allowing" this nasty situation to happen. Even the best teachers on the planet can't supervise every single word of every conversation on the playground. In all likelihood, your child's teacher is doing his (or her) very best.

Rather than criticize the teacher, simply say, "We want to bring this situation to your attention." Share the strategies that you and your child have already come up with. Inquire whether the teacher has any further insights or observations about how your child engages with other children that might be helpful for you to know.

- *If physical violence is a threat, talking isn't enough.*

If your child is dealing with verbal bullying ("You're stupid," "You're fat," "So ugly," etc.) the guidelines I just shared can be a good starting point. (To recap: Ask questions, listen, remain calm, invite your child to generate a solution along with your help, speak to your child's teacher to bring the situation to their attention.)

However, if a bully is threatening your child with physical violence ("I'm going to beat you up," "Watch your back," etc.) or is already engaging in physical violence, then having a conversation with your child is not enough. When physical violence is part of the situation, go directly to your child's principal to report what's happening. In some instances, you may also need to go to the police.

- *Be on the lookout for unusual behavior.*

According to StopBullying.gov, "one reason that parents may be unaware of their children's involvement with bullying is that children often do not tell their parents about their experiences."

What this means, of course, is that your child might be the victim of bullying but choose not to tell you about it. Some children feel ashamed to talk about it, or think their parents "won't understand," or worry that their parents will make the situation worse by trying to intervene.

So, be on the lookout for uncharacteristic behavior. Watch for signs like mysterious ailments or frequent tummy aches, requests to stay home from school, skip certain classes, or leave school early (it's been reported that 15% of school absences are related to bullying), or unusual behavior (like tantruming a lot more than usual or acting withdrawn or depressed).

If these issues are coming up and you're trying to figure out why, don't rule out bullying. It could be a factor.

Get informed.

A useful resource on the web for parents, teachers, and school administrators is: StopBullying.gov.

This website provides statistics on the prevalence of bullying at schools, details on high-risk children who are more likely to be bullied (including gay and lesbian children, overweight children, and children who are perceived as "weak" by their peers), tips on how to prevent bullying from happening in the first place, as well as details on cyber-bullying, which, sadly, is a fast-growing problem.

Read up. Get informed. Ultimately: trust your gut.

If you sense that something is "off" with your child, investigate thoroughly to see if bullying might be the cause.

If you suspect that there's a dangerous bullying situation that could escalate into physical violence, take immediate action to keep your child safe.

To re-emphasize what I mentioned at the beginning of this chapter: every teasing / bullying situation is unique and requires a unique solution. Trust your parental instincts, and don't hesitate to seek help from a counselor, therapist, and school officials.

Closing words: From "victim" to "problem solver."

I met with 12-year-old Ashley twice and then did a follow-up visit with the entire family.

At Ashley's second visit with me, she told me that the boys at school were continuing to call her names, like "stupid" and "fat."

Rather than name-call back, or say nothing, her new strategy was to say, "That's totally uncool," in a calm, neutral tone and then walk away to go sit next to a friend.

It worked! The bullies haven't bothered her since. I congratulated Ashley on her approach.

During the family session, I gave Ashley's parents some suggestions to improve their communication with their daughter (like: "Listen more… don't interrupt… stop criticizing and being judgmental… don't overreact…")

Ashley had shared with me (and gave me permission to disclose to her parents) that these were some of the reasons why she didn't feel comfortable communicating much with them. The family had some fun role-playing different scenarios during our session and practicing healthier communication.

Although this bullying experience was very unfortunate, and something that no one should have to endure, ultimately it brought the family closer together.

Ashley no longer feels like a helpless victim, but rather, a strong problem solver who can take care of herself.

CHAPTER TWELVE

*"My child is having trouble adjusting to
a new home / school situation."*

Jed came to see me because his two children (one in high school, age fourteen, the other, age eight) were both having difficulty adjusting to some recent family changes, including moving to a new home across town.

The reason for the move? Dad had just gotten a promotion that required him to move. Also, Dad's divorce had recently been finalized (the divorce settlement included the sale of the family home). The children spent weekends with Mom, who had also moved to another neighborhood after the divorce.

The older child missed his friends from his old school and seemed to be falling behind academically. The younger child missed his old school, too, especially his extra-curricular activities (he had been very involved with the baseball team at his last school). Both children seemed to be struggling with all of the recent changes.

Jed wasn't sure how to help them with these adjustment issues.

Why do children have difficulty adapting and adjusting?

There are many reasons why a child might have a tough time adapting to a new home, school, family structure, or some other lifestyle change.

Three of the more typical reasons that I see in my work are…

1. Not giving your child sufficient notice about an upcoming change.

While working with Jed, one of the things I learned was that he had not given his children sufficient notice that they were moving. Unfortunately, his two children had almost no time to feel their feelings and deal with the sadness of leaving their friends and familiar places. Whenever possible, give your children a "heads up" about upcoming changes, allowing them plenty of time to prepare… with your help.

2. Not giving your child a chance to see, feel or experience what's coming "next."

Fear of the unknown can be paralyzing. It's much easier to make a significant life change when you have a fairly clear sense of what's coming up next. This holds true for children as well as grown ups!

In an ideal world, <u>before</u> the big move across town, Jed would have driven his children to check out their new neighborhood and visit their new school. This family trip would have given both children a chance to see, feel and experience what was coming "next," which would probably have made the transition smoother and less scary.

3. Allowing your own stress to "spill over" to your child.

Jed was feeling pretty stressed about the move himself. He felt overloaded with everything that he needed to do to prepare, as well as his own adjustments to being a single dad. His relationship with his ex was pretty stressful, too.

He unknowingly allowed his own stress to "spill over" to both of his children, because he wasn't managing his own emotions effectively.

Remember: every single day, <u>you</u> set the tone for your children. If you are stressed out about a big change, your children are likely to feel agitated too. If you feel confident and excited about a big change, your children are likely to feel the same way — or at least, feel a whole lot better about it!

Self-reflection.

Got a child who is struggling to adjust to a new home, school, family structure (after a divorce or re-marriage), or some other lifestyle change?

Here are a few questions to help you see how your upbringing, your past, and your personal choices might have contributed to creating this situation...Did I give my child sufficient notice about this change?

- Did I give my child a chance to see, feel, or experience the new [home / school / etc.] before making the big change?
- Did I give my child an opportunity to share his (or her) feelings about the change? If so, did I jump in and interrupt, or did I listen?
- How do I feel about this change? Happy? Sad? Stressed? Frustrated? Defeated? Elated? A little of everything? Is my child mirroring my own emotional state?
- How have I been managing my own emotions in dealing with this change? (For example: if you are feeling exceptionally stressed out, have you been resorting to binge-eating or binge-watching TV for hours on end as a way to "cope"? If so, has your child witnessed you behaving this way?)

Finding solutions.

If your child is having difficulty adjusting to a new situation, an important first step is to...

Listen, listen, listen.

Go for a walk with your child, or sit together on a comfy couch, and ask an open-ended question like, "How are you feeling about your new [home / school / etc.]?" Assure your child, "You can be totally honest. I won't be upset or hurt, no matter what you say."

Let your child speak. Listen without interrupting.

If your child describes a specific problem, like not having any friends at a new school, resist the temptation to dish out an instant solution or command ("Well, you should walk up to kids and ask if you can play!").

Instead, prompt your child with more questions, like "How do you feel about that?" and ultimately, try to guide your child into coming up with a solution on his (or her) own. ("What do you think would be a good solution?" "What would you like to try?")

If you can help your child to generate a solution on his (or her) own, that will be far more empowering for your child than you doling out the "marching orders," so to speak.

Even if you don't come up with an immediate solution, simply inviting your child to share his (or her) feelings honestly — while you listen without interrupting — can be so healing.

Continue having "check in" conversations during the weeks and months after the big change takes place to see how your child is doing.

On top of that, I strongly suggest that you…

- Get involved in your new community.

Join clubs. Organize a block party. Host a backyard picnic or potluck to bring the neighborhood together. Seek out people who have children the same age as yours, if possible. As your children see you getting involved and meeting new people, they are likely to feel more inspired to follow in your footsteps.

- Help your child to stay connected with old friends.

Encourage your child to keep in touch via phone, email, letters, or even face-to-face visits when possible. Your child might also invite old friends over to spend a weekend or vacation at your new home. By doing this, you are teaching your child that important relationships don't have to end just because you move.

- Keep consistent, familiar routines in place.

As much as you can, keep your child synced into the same routines that he or she was used to in the "old" home. Same bedtime. Same wake-up time. Same family rituals (like meatless Monday dinners). Same rules and chore-chart on the fridge. This familiarity can be comforting to your child and provide a sense of security in the midst of all the changes.

Note: where parents are living in separate households (which means that the child has two homes), work with your ex-partner to make sure that, from a parenting standpoint, you are both on the same page. The same rules should apply in both homes. Consistency can give your child a deeper sense of security.

- Keep your own stress levels in check.

This holds true all the time, every day, but especially during times of change and upheaval. Take extra-special good care of yourself.

Eat well. Work out. Watch funny movies and laugh deeply. Sleep consistently. Discharge negative emotions in private (by, for example, pounding a pillow in your bedroom with the door shut). Model the highest level of "self-care" that you can, and it is likely to rub off on your children.

- Remind your children: "You are loved always."

Above all else, this is the most important message that you can impart to your children:

"You are loved always. No matter where you live, what you do, or who you spend time with.
Yes, you're not going to the same places that you used to go to, and you're not seeing the same people (friends, teachers,

neighbors) that you used to see, and it's OK to miss them. That's understandable.

But know that I love you, and no matter where you are, or who you are with, I'm confident that you will be just fine, and do just fine. I am here for you, always. I love you, always."

Be a role model who models the message that…

"Your environment and external circumstances don't define how you feel or how well you do.

<u>You</u> decide how you feel. You can choose to feel good about yourself and to make the best of any situation, and to do well, no matter where you are."

- Be patient.

Be patient with your child and yourself. Know, too, that different children adjust to new situations at different paces. Try not to compare one sibling to another (definitely avoid saying things like, "Why can't you say 'hello' to kids at school and make new friends like your brother? He's doing fine!").

In time, if you keep consistent routines in place, keep your stress levels in check, and keep modeling healthy, well-adjusted behavior, your child is likely to follow in your shoes.

Closing words: New home, same routines, happier children.

Jed spoke with his ex-wife and together, they made an effort to keep their children's routines, rules and consequences the same in both households. They were not always 100% successful with this, but Jed noticed that the more consistency his children experienced in both households, the less anxious they seemed.

Through our sessions together, Jed began to realize that he was holding onto some unresolved "guilt" about the divorce. Driven by guilty feelings, he would find himself being extra lenient with his children, relaxing the rules, giving out treats, taking his children out shopping for toys, and so on.

"I'll stop doing that once they're more settled," Jed promised. I urged him to parent differently.

"Don't try to buy their happiness. It doesn't work," I explained. "Instead, give them lots of hugs and attention and quality time with you. That's what they really need."

I encouraged Jed to let go of the guilt and other negative emotions that he had been bottling up inside by pounding a pillow using a towel with a knot tied on one end — it's one of the most effective techniques for emotional release.

I urged him to remember that divorce doesn't mean you've "messed up" or that you've "wrecked" things for your children. Not at all. But your children need you to be especially strong, calm, and consistent during this time.

If you are navigating a big change — like a job loss, job change, divorce, or new home — and worrying about the impact on your children, my words for you are the same words that I shared with Jed during our last session together:

"Your job is not to beat yourself up over this change. That's not necessary, and it's not helpful or productive for you or your children.

Your job, right now, is to be kind to yourself, believe in yourself, and be the best parent you can be.

As long as your children have your love, your support, and your role modeling to guide the way, they are likely to be OK."

CHAPTER THIRTEEN

*"My child 'hates' me.
I'm heartbroken."*

Paula's 12-year-old daughter had just done (or rather, said) the unthinkable.

"I hate you, Mom!"

And it wasn't the first time.

"I feel like my heart is shattered into a million pieces," Paula told me during a session, tears streaming down her cheeks. "When I hear those words come out of my child's mouth, I lose it. I start yelling because I'm so hurt. It's awful."

I encouraged Paula to tell me more about the situation. It wasn't pretty.

"My 12-year-old has told me she 'hates' me several times. Now my younger one [7 years old] has also started saying that to me. More than once!"

Paula wants to know what's the best way to handle this situation without angrily "blowing up" or breaking down in tears in front of her children.

She also wants to understand why on earth this is happening. She can't understand why her children are speaking to her so rudely, when she has done nothing but love them since the day they were born!

Why do children lash out and say hurtful things like, "I hate you!"?

Here's a short answer:
When children lash out and speak disrespectfully, it is because they have been taught that they can engage in this kind of behavior, consequence-free (meaning, "Mom yells like that all the time, so I can too!" or "I can say things like that because Dad never gives me any consequences when I'm rude. Anything goes!")

As with just about every behavior issue under the sun, it all comes back to you.

Your behavior. Your communication style. Your parenting style. Your role modeling in the home and out in the world.

Again: when I say, "It starts with you," I'm not assigning blame or shaking a nagging finger in your direction. I'm simply reinforcing the point that you are the single most influential figure in your child's life.

Your child has learned certain life lessons from you already. Many terrific lessons, most likely! And perhaps a few not-so-terrific ones. In some instances, certain lessons need to be "un-learned" and replaced with better ones. This is definitely one of those instances! And you have the power to do just that.

Finding solutions.

If from time to time, your child says hurtful, mean things to you, consider following these guidelines:

- Use an "I hate you!" incident as a teaching opportunity to reinforce why certain rules exist.

Here's an example: Paula's 12-year-old daughter got invited to a sleepover on the weekend and asked her mom if she could go.

Paula's response was, "No, you've already had a sleepover this month and that is the limit."

Ideally, your child already knows that she has a limit of one sleepover per month. (You explained this clearly and created a rule chart that's posted on the fridge, or somewhere else just as visible. There's zero confusion about the household policies.)

Ideally, you've already explained why this particular rule is in place too. (You've given your child a reasonable explanation. Not just, "Because I said so.")

Unfortunately, in Paula's home, neither of these "ideal circumstances" were the case. Paula had not educated her daughter about the sleepover rules, so her daughter was understandably upset, feeling like the "victim" of an unjust situation, which contributed to her inappropriate outburst ("I hate you!").

If this type of situation arises with your child — and your child says "That's not fair!" or "Why is that the rule?!" or "You're so mean, I hate you!" — stay calm. Rather than screaming right back and escalating the situation further, use this moment as an opportunity to explain (or re-explain) why certain rules exist:

"One sleepover a month is all that your schedule will allow. We need to spend at least one weekend a month visiting your grandfather and grandmother, and I want you to be home on the other weekends, so you can get enough sleep, and so that we can be together as a family."

Explanations like this one are necessary because they show the rationale behind your thinking. When you explain why a rule exists, your child is more likely to comply. Simply saying, "Because I'm the parent!" is not enough. You need to give your child an explanation that s / he can make sense of, something that is logical and reasonable.

- Set consequences for rudeness and hostility.

By now, hopefully, your child understands that if he (or she) chooses not to complete a homework assignment, skips chores, lies about having brushed their teeth, leaves clothes lying on the floor, etc., there will be a specific consequence for each infraction.

But does your child understand that "rudeness" and "hostile language" are just as unacceptable as, say, lying? If not, now is the time to educate your child.

Calmly and matter-of-factly, say:

"Saying 'I hate you' is unacceptable. Using harsh, hurtful language of any kind is unacceptable.
If you choose to say something like that again, you will [insert age-appropriate consequence, like, "lose your cell phone privileges for one week"]. Do you understand?"

Make sure that your child understands the new rule and the associated consequence.

And of course, if he (or she) uses hurtful, inappropriate language again, apply the consequence that you've stated. Be consistent.

I've emphasized this before, earlier in this book, but it bears repeating: make sure that the consequence you've selected is unappealing enough that your child really doesn't want it to happen again, but not so severe that your child feels unfairly penalized and resents being "punished." The consequence is intended to offer your child a learning experience ("Next time, I'll make a different choice"). It is not intended to be punitive.

I've found that the most effective consequences are ones that involve removing a child's favorite privileges — temporarily removing TV privileges, sleepover privileges, Internet privileges, cell phone privileges, and so on. Your child will want to earn back a lost privilege — and won't want to lose it again! — which provides ample motivation for good behavior.

- Do not explode at your child. Keep your emotions in check.

Hearing your own child say "I hate you" (or something similarly hurtful) is deeply gut-wrenching. It's not uncommon for a parent to burst into tears on the spot, or explode in anger right back at the child.

I know it can be tough, but make an effort to keep your own emotions in check.

It's important for your child to witness you managing your emotions effectively and modeling calm, clear, respectful communication.

You can be firm — "We do not tolerate that kind of language in this household" — without being explosive.

Remember that if you scream, yell, or make a rude retort in response, you are modeling the same behavior that you are teaching your child not to do!

Take whatever emotions you are feeling, like anger ("After all I do for you, working two jobs to support you, this is the thanks I get?!") or guilt ("It's my fault because of the divorce. My kid hates me now.") and put those strong emotions "on the shelf," so to speak. Tuck them away for the time being. Set them aside. Don't discharge them in front of your child. Handle them later.

By temporarily putting strong emotions "on the shelf," you are not pushing your feelings down inside yourself in an unhealthy way. You are internally saying to yourself,

"WHOA. I am feeling really angry right now. But rather than blow up in front of my kid, I am going to stay cool and turn this moment into a learning / parenting opportunity.

Later, when I am alone, I can go for a long run, pound a punching bag or pound a pillow, journal, or do whatever I need to do to release these feelings safely and in a healthy way.

But right now? I'm going to model calm, respectful communication for my kid. That's my job."

Closing words: Clear rules, no guilt.

In working with Paula, a single mom, I learned that she had given her daughters a lot of leeway from an early age to do whatever they wanted.

Why? Lots of reasons, including dynamics that Paula picked up from her own parents, but primarily because Paula felt guilty about the fact that her children didn't have a dad. To compensate, she indulged them and let them "have their way."

Not surprisingly, her two daughters learned, fairly early on, that "rules don't matter" and they engaged in inappropriate behavior and outbursts.

Rather than enforcing age-appropriate consequences for misbehavior, Paula found herself fearfully or angrily shrieking "NO!" at her children — and in doing so, she modeled that loud, angry outbursts are totally acceptable behavior when you are upset.

Through our work together, I helped Paula to understand that (even though a healthy two-parent family is ideal) as a single parent, she could still effectively guide and teach her daughters, and equip them to grow up into responsible, happy adults.

I urged her to safely release the guilt she felt about the fact that her children did not have a dad. (All that bottled-up guilt was not healthy for her or her daughters.)

In addition to working on her own feelings of guilt, Paula's biggest challenge was to begin setting clear rules and then explaining why those rules existed to her daughters.

She created a behavior chart [see pages 158-165 for a sample chart, along with a few more instructions on how to use charts effectively] so that there was zero confusion about the expectations within the household. This chart made a world of difference. Finally, there was some peace and cooperation in the house!

Naturally, it took both children a little while to adjust to the changes. Paula's older daughter kept asking:

"Why? Why do we have to do all of this, all of a sudden?" (A reasonable question!)

To which Paula explained:

"That's an understandable question. I'm so sorry I didn't teach you these rules years ago. We would all be much happier.

But now that I know about them, I must share them with you, and require you to follow them. That's my responsibility as your mom, and it will be yours one day, too, if you choose to be a mom.

I'll go through, one by one, and explain why each of these rules are important..."

Paula made an effort to offer a sensible explanation for each rule, so that her children fully understood why the rule was important.

During our final session together, Paula shared that things were going so much better.

"You know, I think they were hungry for these kinds of rules all along," she confessed. "My girls are doing so much better with more structure at home. I think they like having a confident adult running the house, instead of a mom who yells, feels guilty, and lets things happen haphazardly. We're all happier now."

CHAPTER FOURTEEN

"My child won't talk to me."

Ten-year-old Ryan's mom came to see me with the following dilemma:

"My son clams up whenever I ask him a question that has to do with feelings. He has no problem talking to me about computer stuff or schoolwork. But feelings are off limits. I understand... I was like that as a child, and I'm that way as an adult. But I worry that he has things on his mind or something's bothering him and he's keeping it inside."

Ryan's mom also shared that her other son, who is 14, never wants to talk to her anymore about anything. Period. She wants to know if this is just a teenage phase that will pass.

Why do children "clam up" and refuse to talk?

There are several reasons why this type of situation might be arising.

It is possible that...

- Your child is emulating a "withdrawn" parent.

Do you express your feelings out loud, or are you a "quiet" and "private" person?

How about your spouse? What about other caregivers in your child's life, like a nanny or grandparent? Do they express their feelings?

If your child is surrounded by quiet, withdrawn people who rarely talk about how they feel, your child may pick up on those cues and follow in tune.

- Your child is reacting to a "highly expressive" parent.

Sometimes, children mimic their parents. Other times, they react to how they experience their parents by behaving in a "polar opposite" kind of way. Either way, your child's behavior is a response to your own behavior (and / or the behavior of another caregiver).

If you (or another influential figure in your child's life) are very expressive, very emotional, perhaps even to the point of being "over the top" or "overwhelming," your child might be responding to this emotional intenseness by drawing inward.

- Your child is "withdrawing" as a way of coping with a stressful situation.

If you and your spouse fight in front of your child, he (or she) might withdraw as a way to cope.

Teasing and bullying at school is another situation that can often cause children to withdraw and clam up.

- Your child feels like you "won't listen anyway... so why bother talking?"

This is a common scenario. If your child feels ignored, or knows that you interrupt more than listen, your child might feel like what he (or she) has to say doesn't matter and won't even be heard, anyway. Your child is likely to feel unwilling to speak up.

- Your child is afraid of making a mistake, saying something "wrong," or being painfully compared to others.

Sibling-comparison is often at the root of this dynamic. If your child frequently hears messages like, "Your sister always keeps her room tidy, why can't you?" or "Your brother manages to complete his homework and his chores, what's your excuse?," your child may begin to withdraw and clam up, fearing the pain of "comparison."

Inside, your child might be thinking, "Ugh, I will never measure up... I wish I could just disappear."

- Your child is giving you the "silent treatment" to "punish" or "manipulate" you.

If your child is upset with you, your child could be "acting out" by refusing to speak, knowing full well that it upsets you, and / or hoping that eventually you will "break down" and give the child exactly what he (or she) wants.

This type of manipulative behavior needs to be treated like any other type of inappropriate behavior: Explain to your child that manipulative behavior is not acceptable and that if it happens again, there will be a consequence. Explain the consequence. Post it in writing on a rule chart, or a similar tracking system.

If your child continues to do the "silent treatment," implement the consequence consistently. (By this point in this book, you know the protocol! If you need a refresher, revisit Chapter One for important information on how to apply consequences.)

"Is it 'normal' for teenagers to sulk or be silent and moody?"

While sulky, moody, withdrawn behavior is quite "common" for teens, that doesn't mean it is a "developmental phase."

As a teenager, your child is definitely old enough to understand the difference between appropriate, respectful behavior and inappropriate, disrespectful behavior.

Disrespectful behavior is <u>learned</u> behavior. It's something that your teen has picked up as "OK to do"... from you (and / or another significant caregiver). As always, it all comes back to role modeling: the lessons you teach, the messages you convey.

If your family has healthy communication skills in place from day one — like making eye contact when you talk, giving your children your full attention when you're conversing, keeping your word and following through consistently, holding calm, non-explosive conversations about difficult topics, listening without interrupting, and so on — then your child is likely to display these healthy communication skills throughout their entire upbringing, including the teenage years.

If your teen has <u>not</u> learned these kinds of healthy communication skills, well, then sure — you're likely to have a withdrawn teen on your hands. But as always, learned behavior can also be unlearned. No matter what kinds of messages your child has absorbed up to this point, it's never too late to try to "course correct" and instill healthier lessons. It starts with you... and it can start today!

Self-reflection.

Is your child unwilling to talk to you? If so, here are a few questions to help you see how your upbringing, your past, and your personal choices might have contributed to creating this situation...

1. Am I withdrawn?

If so, is this a personality trait that you picked up from your own parents or upbringing? Do you think you may have passed this quality onto your child?

2. Do my spouse and I fight in front of our child?

If so, where did you learn this behavior? Who are you modeling?

3. Do my spouse and I give our child our full attention when he / she is speaking? Do we listen deeply and make our child feel like what he / she has to say matters?

4. Did my parents give me their full attention when I was growing up?

5. Am I afraid of making mistakes, saying something "dumb," or being criticized or made fun of?

If so, where did you learn to feel this way? What happened to cause you to feel like this? Have you passed these insecurities onto your child?

6. Do I criticize my child or constantly compare him or her to others?

If so, where did you learn to do this? Where is this impulse to "compare" coming from?

7. Do I give too much advice to my child (so much so, that it could be overwhelming?)

If so, where did you learn to do this? Where is this impulse to "fix things" coming from?

Through answering these self-reflection questions, you may find that you need to do some inner healing work in order to be a better role model for your child.

Let's say, for the sake of example, that you've realized that you often felt criticized as a child. Nothing you did was ever "good enough" for your own parents, or at least, it felt that way. Over time, you began to "clam up" and withdraw into your shell, unwilling to speak up for fear of further criticism. Without realizing it, you've passed this exact same tendency onto your own child.

You might hold a quiet, internal conversation with your inner child, and say,

"I am so sorry that you felt criticized over everything you said when you were little — and that you felt like you could never say anything right, and so you became very quiet.

That was so unfair. The truth is that you are very smart and you say lots of smart things and I love listening to you.

I'm your parent now, I love you and I will never criticize you. So keep telling me lots of things. I can't wait to hear them."

If you've never had a dialogue with your inner child before, this kind of conversation may seem "silly," but it's actually one of the most effective ways to resolve old emotional scars, heal and move on.

Remember: when you are healthy and whole, unburdened by wounds from the past, you become an even stronger role model and source of strength for your child. So even if having a dialogue with your inner child feels "silly," at first, just try it! Do it for yourself. Do it for your own child. It doesn't "cost" anything other than a few seconds of your time, and the benefits can be significant.

Finding solutions.

If you have a child who is shy and withdrawn, or unwilling to talk to you, a powerful course of action is for you to set a healthy example.

Model healthy communication skills to the very best of your ability.

This means…

- Make eye contact with your child when speaking.
- Listen with your full attention (no cell phone at your fingertips, no distractions).
- Listen deeply without continually interrupting.
- Ask open-ended questions that prompt your child to keep talking ("How did that make you feel?" "What do you think about that?" "And then what happened next?")
- Avoid the temptation to jump in and "fix" your child's problems, but rather encourage your child to come up with a sensible solution on his / her own. ("What do you think would be a good solution to this problem?" "If a friend of

yours was in this situation, what suggestions would you give to them?")
- Keep your tone calm and level, even when you're feeling a rush of strong emotions. (No angry outbursts.)
- Keep your word about everything, including when you say, "I'll be with you in five minutes." If you tell your child, "I'll be with you soon, you'll have my full attention in a few minutes" and then you forget or ignore your child, that's not a healthy message to impart. Knowingly or unknowingly, you're basically saying to your child, "Whatever it is that you need to tell me doesn't really matter much."
- Be vulnerable and talk about your own feelings. If you are willing to share age-appropriate, honest, stories about your own feelings, struggles, hopes, dreams, fears, challenges, and so on, then your child will be more likely to mirror you. But if you are withholding, your child won't have a model to follow. Lead by example.

Closing words: Interruption-free communication, happier children!

I worked with Ryan's mom individually for a few sessions, and then several times with Mom and Ryan both present.

It was helpful to see Ryan and his mom interacting together. As it turns out, she frequently interrupted him, finished his sentences, or made critical comments about him (comparing him to his older brother). She was not doing any of this intentionally, of course, and often she wasn't even aware she was doing it!

As an outside observer, I had an opportunity to chime in and call attention to these habits.

"Are you aware that you just interrupted your son?..." I would ask Ryan's mom, politely. Then, a few moments later. "Oops, you just interrupted him again. See that?"

This was affirming to Ryan. He felt heard and seen.

Once Ryan realized that my office was a safe place where he wouldn't be criticized, interrupted, ignored or compared to his older brother, his feelings and thoughts just poured out of him. Withdrawn? Uh, not anymore!

Ryan's mom eventually invited Ryan's dad to participate in family sessions, and these were illuminating experiences, too. Ryan's dad had lots of the same habits as mom (interrupting, criticizing, often without realizing it) and had to un-learn this behavior. It was tough for him, at first, as these communication habits were mostly deeply ingrained. In time, though, both parents made huge progress — and Ryan continued to come out of his shell, being increasingly willing to talk to them.

The parents also instituted electronic device-free "family meals" every night, which hadn't been a consistent ritual before. (In the past, everyone just ate in front of the TV whenever they felt like it.)

Having a consistent dinnertime routine created a beautiful ripple effect for the family, even though dad couldn't always participate due to his work schedule.

"It's a lovely time where we all catch up with each other," says mom.

By making a consistent effort to "catch" their own communication issues (like interrupting, criticizing, comparing, completing people's sentences, and talking towards the TV instead of towards each other) and taking steps to put an end to those habits, Ryan's parents were able to change the entire dynamic in the household.

Today, both Ryan and his older brother feel a lot more comfortable talking to their parents.

They know they're going to be heard — so they are willing to share.

CHAPTER FIFTEEN

*"We are going through a divorce.
My child is so upset."*

Theresa's 7-year-old daughter, Jackie, was having a difficult time with the fact that her parents were getting divorced.

Jackie was living with Theresa and visited Dad on the weekends. Her parents were separated but not officially divorced yet. Theresa had filed the paperwork, though, so things were in motion.

There was no question in Theresa's mind that this divorce was necessary. She had tried to work things out with Jackie's dad in counseling, but he was not receptive and actually didn't show up for quite a few of the scheduled appointments.

But now, in the wake of their separation, Dad's negative attitude was leading to some new issues. He would often tell Jackie, "This is all your mom's fault. I don't want a divorce," bad-mouthing Theresa in front of their daughter and trying to get Jackie to "pick sides." All of this was just too much for the 7-year-old to bear, understandably so, and she was not coping well.

"Mommy, why can't you and Daddy stay together?" Jackie would ask, choking back tears. When her mom tried to explain, "Sometimes mommies and daddies just can't be friends anymore," Jackie started crying, deeply, and then launched into, "I hate you!"

Jackie also started having fights with playmates and was spending way more time alone in her room than usual.

Theresa began feeling powerless to help her daughter — and felt guilty about being the cause of Jackie's problems. Theresa came to me wondering what to do next.

Guidelines for effective parenting during a divorce.

Nobody "wants" a marriage to end in divorce, but sometimes it happens.

Is it automatically going to be a "devastating" experience for your child? Not necessarily. It will be challenging, of course, like any other major change, but with care and thoughtfulness, you can guide your child through the transition gracefully. It can ultimately be a growth opportunity for both of you.

While my thoughts on divorce could easily fill another whole book, here are a few general guidelines to hold in mind:

- Give your child opportunities to talk about what he / she is feeling. Ask questions. Encourage your child to share honestly. Listen without interrupting.

This is a no brainer, but it bears repeating.

- Resist the temptation to "spoil" or "indulge" your child with new toys, a higher allowance, more privileges, and so on.

You can't "buy" your child's happiness and wellbeing during a divorce, or any other time. But you can give your child plenty of love, hugs, attention, and quality time. Always.

- Don't try to "talk" your child out of feeling … whatever he or she is feeling.

Your child might express an understandable emotion, like sadness, saying something like, "I just wish we could keep living together in one house. I feel sad."

All too often, a parent will leap in and try to "convince" the child that there's no reason to be sad. A parent might say something like, "Don't be sad! Things will be so fun with two houses! You're going to have two homes soon, and two rooms. Won't that be fun! And you'll have two sets of toys as well... one in each room!"

When you do this, it's coming from a place of concern — obviously, you don't want your child to feel anxious or sad! But this kind of "fixing" and "sugarcoating" isn't helpful. Rather than trying to list all the reasons why divorce is going to be awesome, just listen. Then listen more.

Say the honest truth, which is, "It's understandable that you feel sad. I feel sad, too." Then reassure your child that no matter what happens, he / she is deeply loved.

"I will love you always. Our family is going through a change, but my love for you will never change."

Self-reflection.

Here are a few check-in questions to ask yourself if you are in the midst of a divorce:

- Am I keeping my emotions about the divorce in check, or is my sadness and anxiety spilling out and impacting my child?
- Have I been bad-mouthing my ex in front of my child? Or vice-versa?
- Have I been making an effort to maintain our usual household rules and routines (family dinner, consistent bedtime, etc.) during this transition?
- Am I communicating with my ex so that we're maintaining consistency in both households?
- Have I given my child an opportunity to share his / her feelings about the divorce with me? If so, did I interrupt or try to "make" my child feel differently?

- Am I giving my child plenty of attention and quality time? Or am I trying to "buy" his / her happiness with treats and toys?
- Am I giving my child plenty of reassurance during this time, like saying "I love you," hugs, snuggles, and having conversations that make him / her feel safe and secure, no matter what?

Divorce is a major life change, no doubt about it.

Continue to check in with yourself, asking questions like these to make sure you're being the best role model and parent you possibly can, even under unusually stressful circumstances.

In doing so, you are teaching your child an invaluable lesson: Yes, it is possible to be calm, graceful, and strong, even when life gets rocky.

Finding solutions.

Here are a few guidelines to help your child to feel loved and secure during a divorce — and to keep outbursts and "acting out" to a minimum:

- Have the talk.

If you haven't already done so, have a conversation with your child about the divorce.

Before you tell your child about the divorce, though, it is essential that you get your own "emotional house" in order. You don't want to appear grief-stricken, furious, or panicked. You need to present a calm, strong front so that your child will feel as secure as possible.

If some emotions come to the surface while you're talking to your child, that's human, and that's fine. You're not a robot, after all!

But try to remember that right now, in this conversation, you're in the role of "parent." Your job is to care for your child. To do that effectively, you'll need to discharge your emotions before you have the "divorce talk" (by pounding a pillow with a towel that you have tied a knot in on one end, for example, or crying it out privately with the door closed) so that you aren't bubbling over in front of your child, causing even more distress.

Depending on your child's age, you may need to explain what "divorce" means.

If your child is very small, you can keep it fairly simple, saying that:

"Mommy and Daddy will no longer be living together in the same house. We will have two houses / homes."

Reassure your child that they are loved, and will continue to be loved by both of you, and that this divorce is not their fault.

After you've shared the news, ask your child if they have any questions and ask how they feel. Listen. Create a safe space for them to share any concerns or feelings.

- Keep familiar routines in place.

In the weeks and months to come, if your child "acts out," like Theresa's 7-year-old daughter Jackie, treat the inappropriate behavior just as you would at any other time. Yes, the family is going through a transition, but that does not mean that "the rules" no longer apply.

Remind your child about the rules and consequences for misbehavior. Keep your "rule chart" visible. Enforce consequences calmly and firmly.

This may seem "harsh," but it's just the opposite: it's very loving.

By keeping all of the rules and routines in place, throughout the divorce, you will be providing your child with a greater sense of security.

While he (or she) may not say so, your child is likely to actually feel safer and happier with the usual rules and routines in place.

Divorce is a time for exceptional consistency, not a time to let all the usual policies "fly out the window."

- Teach self-care / stress-management techniques.

You and your child might be dealing with some intense emotions during the divorce. That's natural, and this can provide a unique opportunity to teach your child some self-care / stress-management techniques. This might be a big change for you to model what it looks like to "manage emotions" in a healthy, well-adjusted way, even when stressful things are going on.

You could say to your child, "Hey, let's go for a long walk to clear our heads" or if you've got a teenager, perhaps, "Do you feel like punching a punching bag with me at the gym? Let's do that!" You might also say, "I'm feeling a lot of emotions right now and I feel like [writing / journaling / painting / going for a swim] to shift my mood. Do you want to join me?"

One highly effective approach for releasing pent-up emotions is the "pillow-pounding technique." (I've touched upon this technique at various points in this book [like in Chapter Twelve and Thirteen], so that term might already look familiar to you.) The pillow-pounding technique is simple but very effective — it was part of my Ph.D. dissertation research, and I teach it to lots of my clients, because it works!

To do it, go to a private place (like a bedroom or garage) and get a throw pillow and a hand towel. Tie a knot in one end of the towel so that it's sort of like a soft "rope" that you can easily hold onto. Pound the pillow using the knotted end of your towel as you express out loud whatever you're feeling. ("I'm angry!" "I'm frustrated, there aren't enough hours in the day to get everything done!" "I'm mad that my kids don't listen!" etc.) Try not to "control" or censor what you are saying. In this safe, private moment, you can say and feel whatever you need to say and feel. No judgment. Continue pounding until you feel a "shift," a sense of release. Some people describe this "shift" as a feeling of lightness or emptiness — in a good way, like something heavy has been unloaded. A clean feeling. Getting to this "shift" point often only takes a minute or two, although it's different for everyone.

If your child is 4 years or older, you can teach this technique to them. I've had parents find great success teaching this technique to their children. It's a powerful way to discharge negative emotions, safely and privately, so that you can re-emerge into your day feeling unburdened and much, much calmer.

Bottom line: whether you try out this particular pillow-pounding technique or not, this time of transition is an opportunity for you to show your child what it looks like to manage your emotions and take good care of yourself, especially during stressful times.

You'll be instilling healthy stress-management practices that can serve your child throughout all of life's many ups and downs, for decades and decades to come.

Closing words: De-stressing = better parenting.

Theresa's first visit with me was emotionally charged. She was feeling a huge amount of guilt about the divorce, anger at her ex, and even some anger towards her daughter for all of those hurtful "I hate you!" outbursts.

I helped Theresa to safely release her pent-up emotions so that they weren't burning up inside, primarily by using the pillow-pounding technique that I outlined in this chapter.

"I didn't realize until I started pounding the pillow, just how much anger I was holding onto about my soon-to-be ex. I feel so much lighter now," Theresa told me.

(Theresa taught her daughter Jackie the pillow process and Jackie loved it, too!)

Theresa realized, fairly quickly, that by taking steps to release anger and stress, she could be a better, more present parent for her daughter. De-stressing = better parenting.

By "pounding out" negative emotions on a regular basis, she was able to have calm conversations with Jackie instead of feeling on the brink of tears (or yelling) all the time.

In time, Theresa was able to help Jackie understand that the divorce was not her fault, that both her parents love her very, very much, and that it was not her responsibility to "do something" to bring her parents back together or get them to change their mind about divorcing.

Theresa tried to use the divorce as an opportunity to teach her daughter an even deeper "life lesson" about self-care, self-love, and resilience:

No matter what is going on around you, there is always a way to be happy and enjoy your life.
You can learn how to release your feelings in a healthy way. You can learn how to speak calmly even when you're stressed. You can love yourself and take good care of yourself, always.
Under any circumstances, you can find a way to thrive.

It's too soon to say how this divorce will impact Jackie once she's all grown up, but based on the huge work that her mom has done, I'm guessing Jackie will be just fine.
More than fine, actually. A strong, confident, amazing young woman who is well equipped to navigate life's ups and downs.

CHAPTER SIXTEEN

*"I keep losing my temper with my child.
I don't know how to stop!"*

Beth, mother to 6-year-old Carl, has come to realize that raising her voice and yelling at her son doesn't trigger the behavior changes she wants. If anything, it makes things worse.

"I love my son so much," she tells me during our first session. "But when he misbehaves and throws tantrums when he doesn't get his way, I explode in the heat of the moment. But the more I rant and rave, the more Carl rebels and sinks into deeper disappointment over not getting his way."

I ask Beth to describe what happens in those moments where she "explodes."

She can't quite put it into words.

"I honestly don't know. I'm not a loud person or anything like that. I feel like I have pretty good self control, most of the time. It's like something snaps in me when my son is throwing a tantrum or being so uncooperative. I just... blow up!"

I ask Beth if she has any techniques that she uses to manage her emotions throughout the day, in other places, not just at home. She tells me she's not sure.

Beth's situation is quite common.

Parenting sometimes pushes buttons — a parent's buttons. When that happens intense emotions can build up inside of you like hot steam inside a kettle. If you don't know how to release those emotions in a safe, healthy way, invariably you "blow."

Unfortunately, that kind of outburst is likely to happen in front of your children, which can be harmful to their development and send a poor message.

Beth confirms that she does not want to be "that kind of mom" for her son. She wants to be a better role model, modeling patience and managing her emotions. She just doesn't know how. We've got some work to do…

Self-reflection.

Do you have a tendency to "blow up" at your children when you feel irritated or annoyed at them or because, for example, they're being uncooperative?

Here are a few questions to help you see how your upbringing, your past, and your personal choices might have contributed to creating this situation…

- Did my own parents yell explosively when I was growing up, or did they model patience and the ability to manage their feelings?
- Did my own parents have any stress-management practices or techniques (like working out, meditating, journaling, pounding a pillow or punching bag, etc.) that they modeled for me?
- What is filling up my "stress tea kettle" the most these days? Do I get particularly stressed out at work, during my commute, after talking to my spouse about finances, worrying about the future, or…?
- When I feel the urge to "blow up" at my kid, what's going through my mind at that exact moment? (For example: "You're so ungrateful, you little brat!" or "I ask nothing of you, except this one little thing! Why won't you just cooperate?!" or "You're so lazy! Just do your chores!")
- Why is "that" specific line of dialogue running through my mind? Why is "that" specific issue so frustrating to me? Does it remind me of something or someone from my past, perhaps in my childhood?

- What are a few things that help me to de-stress? (Example: listening to soothing music, taking a few deep breaths, retreating to a bedroom or private office for a moment, walking, writing, laughing…) Do I make these practices a consistent part of my day, every day? Or do I tend to forget about them and allow stress to build up inside?

Perhaps you "learned" to yell and explode from your own parents or caregivers. Perhaps not.

No matter what your upbringing or family history might be, the legacy of verbal violence and explosive outbursts can stop with you. **A new era can start with you.**

Perhaps you manage your stress levels pretty effectively in most situations, just not at home with your children. Perhaps not.

No matter what your current self-care and stress management habits may be, **you can always learn to do better.**

You can learn how to manage your emotions effectively so that the urge to "blow up" simply doesn't arise in the same way that you may be feeling it now.

It's all possible. It starts with you!

Finding solutions.

If you have a tendency to blow like a volcano on a fairly regular basis, here are some steps you can take to keep your emotions in check and create a more peaceful home-life for your child…

- Unload regularly.

Whether you call it "catharsis," "release," "uncorking," "unloading," or "de-stressing," find a constructive way to discharge bottled-up emotions safely, and regularly. Ideally, at least once a day — more, if you're feeling especially stressed or upset about something.

I've shared several "unloading" techniques in this book, so far, including my personal favorite: the pillow-pounding technique [see Chapter Fifteen for a review].

If you have a tendency to blow, you need to discharge your feelings habitually, safely and often. Consider this just the same as brushing your teeth or drinking water, or going to the bathroom — mandatory self-care to keep you emotionally healthy and to keep your stress-tank levels low, not brimming so high that you need to blow!

Also, if you find yourself thinking, "Oh that's silly. I'm really not a 'stressed' person. My life is fine!," do an unloading exercise anyway. Once you get in there and start unloading, you might be surprised by how much stored-up emotion (fear, anger, guilt, resentment, anxiety, etc.) you need to let out!

- Manage your child's disappointment with a three-step approach: acknowledge, reassure, propose an alternative.

Often, children throw tantrums when they're frustrated about not getting what they want — a toy, a trip to the movies, a playdate, a favorite snack, your undivided attention, etc. They fuss and yell. Then you yell. Then they become even more upset, because now they're scared, uneasy, and disappointed. It's an unpleasant cycle.

I've found that an effective approach, when managing a disappointed child, is to: 1. Acknowledge their disappointment. 2. Offer reassurance. 3. Propose an alternative.

If, say, a child is on the verge of a huge tantrum because dad promised we'd all go to the movies, but now he's stuck in traffic and it's not going to happen, you could say to your child:

"I know you're disappointed. Me too. I was hoping we could all go together. [acknowledge]

Dad loves you, and I love you too, but sometimes things happen that cause plans to change. [reassurance]

Since we're missing the movie tonight, let's make popcorn here at home and work on your puzzle." [alternative]

This communication tends to work very well. By proposing an alternative to the original plan, you're also teaching your child important lessons about flexibility and compromise.

- Let "consequences" do the work for you. No yelling required.

If your child is misbehaving and you need to apply a consequence, you can do so calmly and matter of factly. If the consequence is unappealing enough, that will motivate your child to behave differently in the future (it acts as a deterrent. "I don't want to lose my iPhone privileges again in the future.") There's no screaming and bellowing required on top of an already-unappealing consequence in order for it to "work." The consequence, on its own, is enough.

Imagine a police officer writing up a ticket for a speeding violation. An officer (who's behaving appropriately and professionally, of course!) would say, "You were 10 miles over the limit. I am writing you up a ticket. Since this isn't the first time, your license will be suspended until you attend traffic school and pay a fine," in a calm, matter of fact tone of voice.

The officer knows that there's no need to add yelling into the mix to drive his point across. You messed up. Now you're losing a privilege until you earn it back. Clear and Simple. End of story.

When disciplining your child, try to channel your inner "good cop." Be calm, cool, and collected, and try to adopt a fairly "unemotional" tone. Think: I don't have to yell to get my point across. When necessary, I just need to "state the facts" about the consequence that my child has incurred.

If you apply appropriate consequences consistently, your child is likely to adjust his or her behavior to avoid losing privileges, and in time, the uncooperative behavior is likely to decrease, as well.

Rules and consequences — not yelling and screaming — are the go-to tools that can help you to raise a cooperative child.

Closing words: Not "that kind of mom" anymore!

Beth worked with me in-person and over the phone for several follow up sessions.

She practiced several things, including the pillow-pounding technique, as a means of "unloading" bottled up emotions and regaining her equilibrium throughout the week. She reported that she was surprised by how much she needed to pound the pillow some days.

"Guess I had more 'stuff' bottled up in there than I thought!" she laughed.

She also practiced using the "acknowledge, reassure, propose an alternative" process to soothe her 6-year-old when she sensed he was on the verge of a disappointed meltdown.

"That really helped," she told me. "I think Carl felt so hurt and ignored when his dad canceled a fun family outing that Carl was looking forward to, or when I had to work on the computer instead of playing with him. Maybe he felt like, 'Mommy and Daddy don't care about me.' But that approach helped me to show him that we always love him, even if the plans need to change, or even if we can't give him our full attention in an exact moment. When I tried that approach, he seemed so much calmer, most times. The tantrums are definitely happening way less."

I congratulated Beth on taking steps to keep her own emotions in check, and for modeling calm, rational, even-keeled communication for her son.

Beth's fears of being "that kind of mom" (the yelling, explosive, uncontrolled kind) are no longer on the table.

She's becoming the kind of mom she has always wanted to be.

CHAPTER SEVENTEEN

"I want to parent my child a certain way, but my child's other parent is not on the same page as me."

When Brenda and her husband Rick tied the knot, they got along well and agreed on most things.

But since becoming parents, something has shifted. They get locked into conflicts about the "right" way to parent their daughter, Cassie, now 8 years old.

"We argue all the time," Brenda tells me. "I feel like we're bringing out the worst in each other. Rick won't come to counseling with me. He says I'm the problem, and that I'm too strict with Cassie."

Brenda admits that when Cassie asks why she must do something, like unload the dishwasher, Brenda yells, "Because I said so!" and then punishes Cassie for questioning her.

"I know yelling is bad," says Brenda. "And maybe I am too strict sometimes. But Rick is totally on the opposite end of the spectrum. He always gives in to Cassie because he doesn't want to upset her. That makes me so mad — it doesn't teach Cassie to take responsibility!"

I explain to Brenda that Rick's permissive parenting style (as she described it) does put Cassie at risk for developing behavior problems. However, her authoritarian style isn't teaching Cassie to make positive choices, either. Both parents need to adjust their parenting approach for Cassie's sake.

Brenda agrees with me, but she's not sure that Rick will get "on board," especially since he's not even willing to attend a counseling session.

She's open to improving her parenting approach, but she's wondering if that's going to make a difference if Rick remains exactly the same, unwilling to change.

"Is there any hope for Cassie if her dad continues to be so lenient?" she asks me.

"Yes, there is," I explain. "Ideally, both parents ought to be on the same page, working to present a 'unified front' to their child. But in situations where that's not possible, here's what can work: as long as one parent has healthy parenting skills, and uses the other parent's behavior as an opportunity to teach, not to bash that parent ("Your dad means well, but letting you stay up after bedtime is not good for you because you'll be tired the next day"), then, although the child may prefer the lenient parent's style, in time he or she is likely to grasp the logic in what the 'healthy' parent says and to rely on that parent."

Is this an "ideal" scenario? No. Of course not. But one healthy, effective parent is better than none at all. And one healthy, effective parent can really make a difference in a child's life.

It might make you sad, frustrated, even grief-stricken that you can't rely on your co-parent to "show up" and parent in the way that your child deserves, but ultimately, you can't "force" them to become a better parent. That's up to them to decide.

All you can do is lead by example — for your child, for the other parent in the situation, for the wellbeing of everyone in your family.

Self-reflection.

If you're in a situation where you want to parent your child a certain way, but your child's other parent isn't on the same page, you might be feeling a lot of emotions.

Sadness. Anger. Frustration. Disappointment. Bitterness. Anxiety. Grief… for starters.

Take a few moments of solitude to reflect on how you're feeling so that you can discharge any bottled-up emotions that need to be released.

(Remember the metaphor in Chapter Sixteen of the tea kettle with hot steam building and building inside until... it's just got to blow? That's <u>not</u> what you want to feel like. You'll want to take steps to discharge the steam and empty your kettle so that you can be a calm, clear-minded, present parent for your child. That's essential.)

Ask yourself the following questions. Chat out loud with yourself if you're alone (in your car, for example) or do some free-writing to get those feelings on paper.

- What am I feeling right now?
- Is this feeling lasting longer than fifteen seconds?
- If so, when have I felt this way before? How far back can I remember feeling this way?

The fifteen second rule.

Why did I bring up the number "fifteen" a moment ago?

Because generally speaking, it takes about fifteen seconds to register what you're feeling, feel it fully, identify it ("I am feeling... really, really sad about the break up") and then allow that intense feeling to pass through you, like water flowing through a sieve. ("I'm still a little sad, but mostly OK now. I can get back to my workday...")

A similar feeling might resurface again later on for another fifteen seconds or so ("I feel really sad again"), but you're not feeling "intense sadness" every single second, every single minute, all through the day. It comes in waves, passes through, the intensity leaves you, then perhaps returns briefly... a bit later.

However...

Sometimes, a situation upsets you in an "unusually strong" way. A powerful emotion rises in you, and rather than passing through after fifteen seconds or so, the emotion seems to get lodged, stuck, burning, perhaps growing stronger, for far longer than fifteen seconds.

When that happens, it's invariably a sign that the emotions you are feeling about whatever you are experiencing in the moment are also "triggering" similar emotions related to something you experienced in the past. This "piggy-back" effect (past emotions tailgating present emotions) amplifies what you are feeling in the present. In this instance, though, your feelings are not just about what is happening in the present. You are also reliving emotions in the present that have been stuffed down (repressed) concerning things that happened in the past.

For example: your co-parent promises to attend a counseling session with you, but then flakes out at the last moment and doesn't show up, offering a flimsy excuse.

You might feel angry or sad for fifteen seconds or so, breathe deeply, then move through it.

But… if your co-parent's flakiness reminds you of your father (who continually broke his promises to you when you were a child, and that left you "emotionally bruised") then the anger you feel towards your co-parent might be amplified times two. It's like all the anger you feel towards your co-parent PLUS all the anger you (still) feel towards your father is swirling together into a super-storm. So you feel intensely angry for a lot longer than 15 seconds. The anger is so "big" and "intense" and doesn't seem to be passing along. Almost like it's "stuck."

That's why — when I work with a client who feels an intense emotion that doesn't seem to subside after fifteen seconds or so — I often ask, "When have you felt this way before?" (I explain that the situation and people involved will probably be different, but the intense feeling will be the same as now: anger, grief, fear, etc.)

Their answer can provide clues as to "why" they are so sad (or incredibly mad, or grief-stricken, or bitter, etc.) which can help us to work towards forgiving whoever bruised them emotionally, in the past.

Forgiveness doesn't mean that what someone did was "OK," of course. It just means you're choosing to let it go, let it out, let it pass through you, so that you don't have to carry around that painful burden any longer.

Finding solutions.

Back to the topic at hand: how to be an effective parent <u>even when</u> your co-parent or spouse isn't willing to improve his or her own parenting skills, make necessary changes, uphold the household rules, or create a unified, consistent parenting-front for your child.

- Be a terrific role model.

This goes without saying. Ideally, both parents (or "all" parents, if your child is dividing his or her time between multiple households with multiple couples or spouses or stepparents) would be on the same page about rules, consequences, communication approach, supervision level, values, and so on.

When this isn't the case, it is more important than ever for <u>you</u> to be a stellar role model.

One healthy role model (you!) can really impact your child's life, even if he or she is not present with you 100% of the time.

- Turn "ineffective parenting" moments into "teachable moments."

If your child's other parent does something you don't approve of (like "bribing" your child with candy in order to gain their compliance, or being overly lenient and saying, "Oh, it's OK. You can do your chores tomorrow. Go ahead and watch TV instead…"), you can turn that moment into a "teachable moment" for your child — a chance to re-instill a particular value, to re-teach an important lesson about why we need to behave a certain way, keep our promises, honor responsibilities, and so on.

This "teachable moment" can happen immediately, or it can happen later on, once your child is back in your presence.

For example, you might say to your child:

"I know your dad doesn't require that you take out the garbage, but it is important that you do. Otherwise, you will get in the habit of not doing what you're supposed to do — and that

could mean that you're grades will suffer (if you don't do all your homework), you might get cavities (if you don't brush your teeth), and you may not have friends (if you don't keep your promises).

So I want you to see how important it is to do what I tell you to do — and to do those things, because it's the right thing to do, and it's what's best for you."

Notice how, in the "take out the garbage" example I included just above, you're not "bashing" or "shaming" the other parent or making them into the "villain." You're simply stating, matter of factly, what <u>you</u> require your child to do.

Maintaining this calm, matter of fact tone is vital. Your child doesn't need to see your frustration spilling out (even if you are very, very mad at the other parent!). That's not productive. Your child needs to see you being a healthy role model and teacher. You can accomplish this without directly "bashing" anybody else.

- Forgive... and don't give up hope.

You may need to focus on forgiving your child's other parent for disappointing you, for making your life more difficult than it needs to be, for not being the kind of parent you know they can become.

You've probably heard the old expression "forgiveness will set you free," and while it may sound like a cheesy song lyric, it really is true.

If you are burdened with angry, heavy feelings about your co-parent, you will be a less calm, collected, effective parent for your child. Unburden yourself and let it go.

That doesn't mean that your co-parent's behavior is "OK," and it doesn't mean you should "give up" on him or her

Keep encouraging that co-parent to attend counseling with you. Keep opening the door to having conversations about your child's wellbeing. Keep hope alive.

At the end of the day, you can't ever "force" someone to change. The willingness to change must come from inside of them. It's their choice. But you can support them in making that choice by setting a good example (inspiring them to do better) and keeping the door "propped open" for conversations, counseling, and so forth.

Don't give up hope completely. People can be surprising. You just never know.

One day, your child's other parent might "come around."

Closing words: Forgive and march on.

I coached Brenda over the next few months. (Her husband Rick remained unwilling to join us for coaching, unfortunately.)

Brenda had a lot of anger and sadness about the fact that her husband wasn't willing to get "on the same page" with her parenting-wise, and she was struggling to forgive him.

We focused on strategies to help her release those intense emotions, including using the pillow-pounding technique. [See Chapter Fifteen for a review of this technique.]

She reported back to me that the pillow pounding "wasn't working" because it "makes me feel more mad."

I told her that means it is working, "It's just that your feelings are telling you that you have more pounding to do… more anger to release." That made sense to her, and so from then on, if she felt more mad after she pounded the pillow, she would pound it some more… until she felt calmer inside.

This technique helped her to feel at peace emotionally, so that she could focus on being a strong parent for Cassie, and guide and teach her with confidence and conviction.

She still wishes that Rick would focus on improving his parenting skills, just like she is, and she hasn't given up hope just yet. But even if he never "comes around," Brenda feels empowered knowing what a difference she can make in Cassie's life, in spite of, or despite the discipline differences between her and Rick.

She doesn't need to pound the pillow nearly as much as when we first started working together. But she finds it reassuring to know that the outlet is available to her, any time she needs it.

CHAPTER EIGHTEEN

"My child's grandparent / stepparent / babysitter is spoiling her! Now she is acting out because I'm not as 'nice' as the 'other' grown ups."

Denise and Jim came to see me about something that occurred between their 12-year-old daughter and her paternal grandparents, whom she loves dearly.

"Tracy spent this past weekend with her grandparents," says Denise. "And Jim and I just found out that they bought her a cell phone after we specifically told them we didn't want her to have a cell phone until she was at least 14."

Apparently Tracy had told her grandparents that she really, really wanted a phone, so they said they would buy her one, but told her that she should not use it in front of her parents because it would upset them. (In other words: Tracy's grandparents encouraged her to lie to her own parents!)

Denise and Jim worry that Tracy's grandparents are undermining their authority as parents and being a bad influence on their child.

"We want them to be part of Tracy's life," Denise continued. "And we understand the tendency to spoil grandchildren, but we're worried they're giving Tracy some bad ideas about life."

I understand Denise and Jim's frustration. It's not easy, when you are committed to being a firm, loving, effective parent — modeling good behavior for your child — only to have your efforts undermined by another influential figure in your child's life, like a grandparent, stepparent, babysitter, or even a teacher, mentor or athletic coach.

Before we dig into some potential solutions for this parent-grandparent clash, let's take a look at why "childcare conflicts" can arise...

Why do "childcare conflicts" arise?

In my experience, when conflicts arise between you and your child's grandparents / stepparents / babysitters, etc., it can often be traced back to the fact that...

- You, as the parent, have not researched the parenting / childcare philosophies of these other people. (Or you assume, perhaps incorrectly, that they are "just like you"!)
- You, as the parent, have not clearly informed other adults to whom you entrust your child's care about your rules for watching TV, eating, discipline, etc. (You assume that your child will "fill them in," perhaps? Not likely.)
- You, as the parent, have not thoroughly researched whether these people will follow through with your instructions. (Or they are lying to you about having done so.)

And / or...

- You, as the parent, have chosen to "look the other way" when you see other people (like grandparents) deviating from your guidelines, because you figure, "what's the harm"? (That is, of course, until your child starts misbehaving! Then you want to take corrective action because you realize, "This isn't good.")

Ultimately, as a parent, you are the most influential figure in your child's life. This means that even if other people occasionally veer away from your parenting guidelines, your child is not going to be "spoiled" or dramatically thrown "off track." As long as your child experiences consistency from you at home, occasional "deviations" will probably not throw everything into chaos.

That said, it is your responsibility to make sure that your child is being exposed to the right kinds of role models and caregivers, as well as messages, media, and entertainment. This means doing your "due diligence" to make sure that the other "influencers" in your child's life are on the same page as you.

Having a ten-minute conversation to outline the rules and explain your parenting approach can make a world of difference!

Self-reflection.

Are you finding yourself in a situation where other grown ups in your child's life are "spoiling" him or her, or modeling behavior that you don't approve of?

Here are a few questions to ask yourself:

- Have I clearly outlined my rules regarding nutrition, bedtime, TV, video games, discipline, haircuts, tattoos, etc. to all of the other caregivers in my child's life, as well as why these policies are important for my child's wellbeing?

Grown ups, just like children, rarely like being told to "just do what I say." People of all ages tend to respond a lot more wholeheartedly to instructions when they are offered a logical "reason" for why something needs to happen.

- If one of my child's other caregivers does something that I don't like, does my annoyance feel "in proportion" to the situation, or out of proportion?

(Example: If Grandma takes my child out for pasta and then pizza, both in the same weekend, even after I said, "please minimize processed flour products and dairy," do I feel mildly annoyed and quickly get over it, or do I completely flip out?)

- If my annoyances / anger feels "out of proportion" to the situation (i.e., amplified, exaggerated), why might that be? What is causing such intense emotions to boil up for me?

(Am I being "triggered" by some unresolved drama / trauma / emotional bruising from my past?)

- Am I caught in a "power struggle" with my kid's other caregivers?

(Are the rules that I am insisting upon really all about my child's wellbeing, or am I "acting out" unresolved emotions connected to my upbringing or perhaps even my in-laws?)

- Would it be beneficial for me to learn how to "relax" my rules somewhat, while still trying to bring all of my child's caregivers onto the same page?

Nobody is going to parent or guide your child in "exactly" the same way that you do… and it's possible that nobody will live up to your high standards!

While striving for consistency and excellence is terrific, it's equally important to relax and accept that you can't micro-manage every minute of your child's life. Nor is that necessary or healthy.

In many instances, a bit of humor and levity can be a very good thing — and it's healthy for your child to see you modeling "flexibility" and "compromise," rather than being outrageously rigid when things don't go as you'd like.

Finding solutions.

If you're frustrated about the behavior of your child's other caregivers, worried about their negative influence on your child, and / or want to prevent miscommunication in the future, here are some steps you can consider taking…

- Put your parenting plan in writing and share it.

It's tough to educate other people about your parenting rules / approach / philosophy if you don't exactly know what it is, or how to articulate it yourself!

Either on your own — or with your spouse / partner / co-parent — take some time to clarify your parenting plan and put the key details in writing.

You might want to write down a few sentences about your philosophy ("We believe…"), a list of your core values, a list of basic rules and associated consequences, (not a huge list, maybe the 5 to 10 most important things to know) along with your phone numbers (in case the caregiver needs to reach you with a question or concern) and a name and number for an alternate contact if both of you are unavailable.

Just like the "behavior chart" that you are (hopefully!) using with your child, putting policies "in writing" is very helpful for grown ups, too.

- Go through the plan in person — and explain the reasoning behind your policies.

Handing a babysitter, stepparent or grandparent a written-out plan is great — but invariably, it's not enough.

It's helpful to walk through the plan together, ideally in person, explaining why certain policies are in place so that the other caregiver understands your reasoning.

This conversation doesn't have to be "emotional" or "intense" or "long." A ten-minute chat should cover it. Finish up by affirming that you trust and appreciate this caregiver.

You could say something like:

"Thanks for letting me walk you through our parenting plan. I trust your judgment and I'm grateful you're in my child's life.

We're not aiming for rigid perfection here, but I'd appreciate it if you could keep these rules 'in full effect' while my child is with you, as much as possible.

I've found that the more consistency my child receives from parents and other influential grown ups like you, the better he / she behaves, and the happier he / she feels."

- Pay attention to your child's behavior to spot potential issues / inconsistencies.

If — after spending a weekend at an aunt's house, for example — your daughter begins to protest her 8pm bedtime, saying, "But Aunt Lisa lets me stay up until 9!" that's a pretty clear sign that Aunt Lisa has not been upholding your policies consistently.

You can use this as a "teachable moment" for your daughter — a chance to reinforce why a particular rule (or value, lesson, message, etc.) is reasonable and important.

You could say:

"I know Aunt Lisa lets you stay up later, and that you like that, but you need to go to bed at 8pm because otherwise you are tired in school the next day and then you don't learn as well. So it is important that you go to bed at 8pm every night. Do you understand?"

You might follow by saying:

"I will speak to Aunt Lisa about this so that she understands the rules for next time. Aunt Lisa cares about you and I know she wants you to get plenty of sleep too."

Then, do exactly that.

Clarify your policies with Lisa using a calm tone. (Remember: it's possible that she simply forgot about your daughter's bedtime. There's no need to go into attack-mode or blow the situation out of proportion.)

Of course, if situations like this continue to arise, and Lisa is obviously ignoring your wishes, consider choosing a different caregiver for your child.

A few guidelines that specifically pertain to stepparents...

Many stepparents make the mistake of parenting a stepchild too soon after marrying the biological parent.

At this point, stepparents are often like strangers to their stepchildren. Little or no bonding has occurred and this new relationship can be threatening to the child. This is why some stepchildren rebel and act out.

This type of conflict can be avoided if the potential stepparent is introduced to the stepchild long before marriage and if they share experiences together, like social and recreational activities. This allows the two of them to begin to bond. Prior to marriage, the biological parent and stepparent should also agree on a parenting style (and ideally, confer with the child's other parent to make sure that everyone is on the same page.)

If you're unhappy with how your ex (or your ex's new spouse) is parenting your child, and if they seem unwilling to work with you harmoniously, review the previous chapter in this book [Chapter Seventeen: "I want to parent my child a certain way, but my child's other parent is not on the same page as me."] for suggestions on how to parent effectively even when your child's "other" parents are not in synch with your approach.

To emphasize a vital point from the previous chapter, once again: it is so important that you refrain from "bashing" or "bad-mouthing" your child's other caregivers (including exes and stepparents) when those grown ups do something you don't approve of.

Rather than saying something like, "Oh, your stepmom said that? Well she's an idiot and she's got no idea what she's talking about! That's not how we do things here!" turn the situation into a calm "teachable moment" for your child.

Without letting your frustration bubble out, calmly reinforce why your policies are sensible and important. Rather than bashing the other adults in your child's life, focus on being the best role model that you can be.

Closing words: Clear policies, more harmony.

During our initial session, I recommended to Denise and Jim that they have a chat with Tracy's grandparents about the "secret cell phone purchase" incident.

I urged them to be gentle and gracious when broaching this topic with the grandparents, not combative. Tracy's grandparents did not intend to do any harm. Their actions were not appropriate, but not malicious, either. They just wanted Tracy to be happy.

I encouraged Denise and Jim to explain that they love and appreciate the grandparents so much, but the fact is that purchasing a phone against their wishes (and then encouraging Tracy to lie about it) is just not OK and must not happen again.

I also encouraged Denise and Jim to explain to Tracy that her grandparents love her very much, and that they meant well, but that lying is never OK, and that if they (her parents) give an instruction (like: "No cell phone until you are 14"), that is the instruction that must be followed. Period.

I advised them to forewarn Tracy that if she tries to manipulate her grandparents (or anyone else) in the future so that she can get her way or wriggle around her parents' rules, she will lose her TV privileges for one week. (Tracy has several shows that she looks forward to watching every week, so this consequence was strong enough to motivate her to behave appropriately.)

A week after my initial session with these parents, we did a follow-up phone session.

They told me that they felt really good about how the two discussions went (one with the grandparents, the other with Tracy.) The grandparents promised not to buy Tracy anything without checking with the parents first, and Tracy understood the lessons that her parents conveyed to her about always following their instructions.

A month later, at our final session, the parents were happy to report that there had been no further incidents when Tracy was under her grandparents' watch. These parents were really pleased about how they had handled this sensitive situation.

Tracy's relationship and bond with her grandparents continues to develop and strengthen. And she's very much looking forward to getting a cell phone… when she turns 14!

CHAPTER NINETEEN

"I have one child who is highly successful and gets praise all of the time. I am worried that my other child feels less loved."

Chris came to see me because his 7-year-old daughter, Molly, was having a hard time and he was worried about her.

"Last week Molly pounded her fist on the kitchen table so hard and couldn't stop crying. I was really worried that she was going to injure her hands."

The reason for Molly's meltdown? Her older sister, Jena, had just made honor roll at school. Her mom was so proud of her that she took her shopping for a dress she's been wanting. Molly was not invited to come along.

"A few words of praise from her mom would have made Molly ecstatic," said her dad. "She works hard to be as smart as her sister and to do as well in school. She's making progress, but that's not enough to get praise from her mom — which is what she really craves."

I asked Chris if he had been able to speak to Molly's mom about this problem.

"She says I'm overreacting and that Molly is usually well-behaved, so we shouldn't cater to this 'juvenile, attention-seeking behavior'," he explained to me.

It was clear to Chris (who as a child had been favored by his mom) that Molly's mom was partial to her older sister, always touting her accomplishments and rewarding her with gifts.

Chris wanted help with making sure that Molly did not feel overlooked or become damaged by this unfair treatment.

"I was the 'golden boy' of my own family," Chris went on to explain. "I saw how damaging that was to my siblings' self-esteem. I don't want the same dynamic to happen with my kids. I want to make sure that both of my daughters feel special and loved, and really feel that we're proud of them."

Why do parents develop "favoritism" for one child over another?

If you feel some favoritism towards one of your children, or if your spouse or co-parent does, it doesn't mean that you're a "bad parent." But it is a pattern that's worth investigating, for the benefit of both / all of your children.

There are many reasons why a parent may favor one child over the other.

A few common scenarios are...

- Favoring one child because he / she is just "easier" to parent.

(Less argumentative, less rambunctious, more smiley and sweet-natured.)

- Favoring one child because he / she is helping you to live out certain fantasies from your own childhood or past.

(Example: "I wanted to be a ballerina, but was never good enough. Now my child is a ballerina and my childhood desire to be a ballerina is vicariously being fulfilled.")

- Favoring one child because they "remind" you of someone you love or miss.

(Example: I once counseled a mother of three who favored her older daughter. In counseling, it became clear that this mom had not fully grieved the loss of her own mother — and her daughter reminded her of her late mother. That's why she favored this child.)

- Favoring one child because of a strong lesson or message that you received from your own parents — a message that you are now consciously or unconsciously instilling into your own child through your words and actions.

(Example: "Nothing matters more than winning! If you succeed in athletics, you'll have every college begging you to attend and the world is your oyster!")

- Favoring one child because of a biological connection, perhaps unconsciously treating this child differently than his / her adopted siblings or step-siblings from a new marriage.

And the list goes on…

If you know where your favoritism is coming from — past experiences, unresolved emotions, voids that need to be filled, messages from your own parents, etc. — that's great. Self-awareness is always helpful!

But even if you're not quite sure what's driving your behavior, you can still stop. Just like tossing a pack of cigarettes in the trash can, or pouring a glass of purified water instead of a sugary soda, you can make personal choices, starting right now, to adjust your behavior and create a healthier environment for your children.

The first step in this process is to forgive yourself for feeling… whatever you are feeling.

If you feel an extra-special bond with one child, and not another, guess what? That's OK. You are human, and human beings have certain likes, dislikes, and preferences. We're drawn to certain personalities and not others. That's natural. You don't need to "beat yourself up" over it.

But… a big but… feeling an emotion and then acting on that emotion are two very different things.

It's perfectly OK to feel something without allowing that feeling to influence your words and actions.

You can <u>feel</u> more bonded to one child, at least at this point in your life (Who knows? Your feelings might change one day!), without allowing those feelings to outwardly influence your parenting style with both children.

In other words:

You can choose to parent in a balanced, fair manner — <u>giving love and attention in equal amounts</u> to all of your children — no matter how you might be "feeling" inside.

Self-reflection.

Are you consciously (or unconsciously) giving one of your children extra love, attention, and affection? Is one of your children feeling left out, ignored, or constantly "in the shadow" of a "golden" sibling who seems to do everything right?

Here are several questions that might help you to clarify why this is happening for you (though, as I emphasized before, knowing "why" is not a pre-requisite for changing your behavior. You can choose to change your actions even if you're not 100% sure "why" this scenario is happening.)

- Do I feel a stronger bond with one of my children over the other? Why is that?
- Did I experience a similar dynamic when I was growing up?
- Has anything happened recently that could be contributing to my feeling this bond?
- Do I focus more attention on one child over another?
- Did I get more (or less) attention than my sibling/s did when I was a child?
- Is my "favorite" child filling a "void" within me? Am I vicariously living out my own fantasies through this child?
- Has anything happened recently that could be contributing to my feeling this void?
- Do I discipline one child less than another?

- Did I experience a similar dynamic when I was growing up?
- How do I feel when I'm around [insert name of favored child]?
- Why do I feel that way around that child?
- How do I feel when I'm around [insert name of unfavored child]?
- Why do I feel that way around that child?
- Am I willing to set my feelings of favoritism aside and make an effort to parent more fairly, giving equal amounts of love and attention? Why is it important that I do so?

Finding solutions.

Favoritism may seem somewhat "innocent," compared to other parenting dilemmas, but it can be quite harmful.

The child who you don't favor is likely to suffer emotionally (with low self-esteem, for example, wondering, "What's wrong with me? What am I not doing right?" "Why doesn't Daddy love me as much?"). That child may very well develop academic problems (low self-esteem can lead to under-performing at school, test anxiety, and an overall lack of confidence), as well as anger issues (venting in aggressive, potentially harmful ways, for example, like little Molly pounding her fists on the table until they were nearly injured), and other problematic behaviors.

These issues, if left unaddressed, tend to follow the unfavored child into adulthood and can impair relationships and cause self-esteem to erode even further.

What many parents don't realize is that favoritism affects all of the children in the family, not just the unfavored one. By playing favorites, you're also placing an unfair amount of responsibility on your "golden child," who now feels pressured to fulfill your unmet emotional needs — to be the best ballerina, the perfect student, the golden athlete, or to comfort you through the loss of your own mother or husband, to be happy all the time so they can bring warmth to your life, and so on.

It's not healthy to put children in the position of having to fill their parents' unmet needs.

Of course, you will never treat each child exactly the same. Every child is different and has unique needs, and each child is going to touch you in a different way.

That's OK — as long as your parenting motive is one of unconditional love, and is not colored by your own unresolved issues or unmet needs.

The best "solution" going forward is quite simple:

Treating all of your children with love, attention, and affection, in equal amounts.

This means spending quality time with all of your children in equal amounts.

Praising your children (for their different but equally awesome abilities) in equal amounts.

Hugging your children and telling them you love them, in equal amounts.

Celebrating progress and achievements in equal amounts.

Also, disciplining each child when needed (no "looking the other way," sometimes.)

It may be helpful to apologize to your children, too, letting them know that you're adjusting your behavior and making some changes. Reassure them that things are going to be different — and keep your word.

You can say something like this:

"I've realized that I've been spending a lot of time with [name of child] lately, but not as much one-on-one time with you [other child].

I've also noticed that I have a tendency to praise [name of child] a lot for her achievements, and that I've been leaving you [other child] out even though you're doing great work, too.

That's my mistake, and that changes today.

I want both of you to know that I love you so much. I am so proud of both of you. I am so happy to be your mom / dad.

You are both so talented and special, and from now on, I'm going to make sure you both feel just how proud I am... of both of you!"

This kind of honest "apology" is very powerful for your children to witness.

In addition to reassuring your children that things are going to improve, you're also imparting a valuable lesson:

"Sometimes people realize that how they're behaving is not correct, and that it's time to make a change. That's what I'm doing right now."

Closing words: A surprising phone call, a breakthrough, and... progress.

During my initial meeting with Chris, I suggested that he encourage 7-year-old Molly to share with him what she was feeling at the time that she banged her fists on the table, so that she could verbalize to him how she felt and in doing so, release some of her frustration. (I also encouraged Chris to introduce Molly to the "pillow-pounding" tool for anger management. See Chapter Fifteen for a review of that technique.)

I also suggested that he assure Molly that her mother loves her very much, and that — without badmouthing the mom — he could tell Molly that it's not fair how her mom favors her older sister, and that all children should be treated equally, because they are all loved equally. This way, Molly could feel as if she was heard and understood — even if it was only by one parent. Chris said he felt relieved when he left my office, like he had some tools to help Molly to feel better and to build her self-esteem.

A week later, Kate, Chris's wife called me. She said Chris had told her that he had come to see me and that it was very helpful. She said she was calling to request an appointment for herself because she needed help.

I saw Kate a few days later. She explained that the day before she had contacted me, she received a call from Molly's teacher which stunned her. Apparently the teacher informed Kate that Molly said she wanted to come and live with her (the teacher.) Molly also asked the teacher if she would be her mommy. When the teacher asked what this was all about, Molly said that her real mommy doesn't love her, she only loves her big sister — "Because my mommy never says nice things to me like she does to my big sister, or buys me things or takes me to my favorite places like she does my big sister."

This information from the teacher hit home for Kate — and she knew she needed help. She no longer denied her favoritism of Molly's older sister. She felt guilty, like she was not an effective parent.

Over the next few sessions we focused on identifying why Kate unfavored Molly, and why she wanted to do everything for her older daughter and spend all her time with her.

In time, Lisa realized that when Molly was born, she had a natural instinct to protect her older daughter and make sure that she didn't feel left out — because that's what had happened to her as the older child in her own family. She felt "left out" and "replaced" when her siblings were born.

In this way, Lisa was compensating for her own emotional bruises from the past, making sure her daughter didn't experience what she did growing up, and making sure that she didn't need to relive her painful childhood experience as the older sibling through her older child.

This awareness offered her great insight. She was able to write a new "script" for herself — to replace the old script that had been driving her parenting choices up till now. Old script: "Don't let your older child feel left out like you felt as a child." New script: "That was then, this is now. I am no longer the older sibling feeling left out, and I don't need to protect my own older child from feeling left out. I can love both my children fully and equally."

And that is what she did.

CHAPTER TWENTY

"I am struggling with something extremely difficult right now (addiction / alcoholism, etc.) Quite honestly: I'm not OK. Can I still be an effective parent for my child?"

Maria came to see me because she was concerned that her alcohol problem was affecting her children.

"It's been a problem for years," she told me. "But I never felt OK about seeking help because to me that meant I was 'weak'."

Maria is what some would call a "high functioning alcoholic." She has a good job, she works out, and up until recently she considered herself a good parent to her children, now eight and fourteen-years-old.

She was also very good at leading a "double life," as she disclosed to me.

Every night when she came home, without fail, she would need to have two bottles of wine. She didn't feel like she was physically addicted to alcohol ("I can go without it for a period of time if I need to") but psychologically she needed her fix. She also needed to drink on certain occasions, like business lunches or dinners.

Sometimes she'd have blackouts after a heavy drinking night. The next day she would have absolutely no recollection of what had happened.

Up until now, she thought she had managed to cover up this behavior from her children, because she always did it alone. She said that her husband knew about her problem, but he felt that there was nothing that he could do about it... and as long as it didn't affect the children (or so he thought) he participated in the cover-up.

The problem is that about a year before Maria came to see me, her husband was diagnosed with a rare form of cancer. He had surgery to remove the tumor and follow-up radiation. For months after that, these parents believed that everything was fine. However, about three weeks ago, Maria's husband learned that the cancer had returned. He underwent further radiation, which unfortunately impaired other healthy parts of his body, including his hearing. The prognosis did not look good.

Maria found that she was now drinking more and more, unable to cope with the anxiety over her husband's condition, and lately, she was having difficulty hiding her habit from her children.

"Sometimes," she said, "if my kids aren't behaving, I use it as an excuse to drink even more."

It was hard for her to admit this next fact, but finally she blurted it out...

"Then I say to the kids, 'You're frustrating me so much that now I need some wine!'"

The children were starting to believe that mom's drinking was their "fault." "Mom, if I hadn't been born," said the eight-year-old, "You wouldn't be drinking."

Maria was ashamed and embarrassed about her behavior, and filled with fear and grief about her husband's condition.

But mostly, she was questioning whether she could still be a good mom to her children, given her current situation and after hearing her eight-year-old's comment, she worried about the impact of her drinking on her child's self-esteem.. That's why, after years of refusing help, Maria found herself in my office... finally willing to talk.

Can you be a "good parent" even if you're battling a big problem like an addiction?

The answer to this question is: it's complicated and it depends on each unique situation.

Here's the unpleasant news:

Alcoholism, or any kind of addictive or extreme behavior, takes its toll not only on the person who is having the problem, but on the entire family as well.

Households tend to be disrupted by chaos and conflict, with anger expressed as rage and even violence. Family members feel like they're riding an emotional roller-coaster, never knowing what mood or state the alcoholic will be in.

Children of alcoholics are prone to experiencing emotional stress. This can trigger problems such as failing grades, dropping out of school, and lack of friends. Older children may go off by themselves for hours, strive for perfection, hoard things and become self-conscious or phobic.

The coping skills that children develop to survive an alcoholic upbringing often cause difficulties later in life. Problems include poor self-image, inability to trust, compulsive behaviors, and difficulties in forming close relationships. It is also not uncommon for adult children of alcoholics to become chemically dependent and / or to marry an alcoholic, themselves.

Early professional intervention is critical to prevent serious impairment.

The most important component, of course, is that the parent who is struggling recognizes that there is an issue and is willing to change.

Here's the good news:

The fact that Maria is aware of the potential harm to her children is a good thing.

The fact that Maria is willing to seek professional help is another good thing.

But she's got a lot of work to do, starting with opening up to her children (in an age-appropriate way) about the situation she's in. That means being upfront and honest. No more lying, hiding, or denying that there's a problem.

Why lying to your children about addiction to "protect them" isn't a good choice.

When children sense that there's a problem at home, but then get told that they're mistaken ("Nothing's the matter, really! Mommy's just under a bit of stress,") they often feel invalidated and doubt themselves ("I guess I got it wrong…") or they suppress their feelings, leading to explosive outbursts and other unhealthy responses later on.

Children must be given age-appropriate explanations about an addiction, be it overeating, excessive drinking, another form of substance abuse, or whatever the issue may be.

For most age groups, you can keep this conversation simple and straightforward.

There's no need to go into a huge amount of detail. This isn't a therapy session or a chance for you to vent — this is you, being a role model for your child, and reassuring your child that you're working diligently to get stronger.

Try saying something like:

"You've probably noticed that I have been [describe your behavior: drinking a lot of wine, eating too much food lately, etc.]. You might be wondering why.

Sometimes, when grown ups feel angry or sad, they do unhealthy things to try to feel better. This is not OK, though. It's hurtful. I know this now, and that's why I am working on [describe how you are changing]."

It's also a good idea to apologize to your child and reassure them that your behavior is <u>not</u> their fault:

"I am sorry if my [reiterate behavior] has upset you. I want you to know that my [behavior] is <u>not</u> your fault.

This is my problem and I am dealing with it in the best way I can.

I love you and it's my responsibility to take care of you and set a good example for you. I haven't been doing a very good job of that lately, but that changes now."

Finding solutions.

Obviously, the best (and only) solution here is to put an end to the addictive behavior — for your own wellbeing and for the sake of your children.
Easier said than done? Yes.
Possible? Also… yes.
My client Maria was receptive to trying to resolve her addictive behaviors, but her basic belief was "once an addict always an addict." That is a perception that many people hold, but I do not. Although there are exceptions (fetal alcohol syndrome, for example, where an infant could be predisposed to addiction if the mother consumed high levels of alcohol during pregnancy) generally speaking, alcoholism is a learned behavior, just like overeating.
Maria agreed that she didn't think she was born addicted to red wine or martinis, for example, (and other clients of mine, who were overeaters, have agreed that they weren't born addicted to ice cream.) Any behavior that has been learned can be unlearned.
Maria quickly began to realize that she was using the alcohol to drown her emotions — her fear of losing her husband, her grief over his illness and potential death, her anger about the unfairness that this was even happening.
"He's only fifty," she said. "And he's such a good man. Such a good dad."
I helped Maria feel safe enough to feel her feelings, and to express them safely and in private. She also realized that when she was a child, expressing feelings was considered a sign of weakness in her family. That's a big reason why she suppressed her feelings by drinking. But because she had been so conditioned to believe that weakness was unacceptable, she even learned to be discreet about her drinking — because that vice, if known, would have been considered a weakness, too.
But then, there came a point when she couldn't keep her drinking a secret any longer. Her addiction took on a more full blown, visible identity.
Maria needed to build an entire "toolkit" of new tools to help her cope with intense emotions without turning to alcohol for

comfort. She found success using the pillow-pounding technique (pounding a soft pillow while at the same time verbalizing her feelings which gave her a sense of release and relief), along with journaling, meditation, forgiveness exercises, and therapy and coaching conversations with me.

Slowly, she began to realize that emotions are not "bad" or an indication of "weakness." Emotions can be felt. Emotions can be released in safe, healthy ways. Emotions can be managed successfully — without requiring alcohol or any other substances to suppress them to tolerable levels.

Maria began to feel stronger, healthier and more alive than ever before.

Her children reaped the benefits of her brave choices and powerful lifestyle changes.

Closing words: Recovery is possible. Progress is possible. Anything is possible.

The "happy ending" to Maria's story may sound like I'm laying out a fairy-tale conclusion and many people would say that it is unrealistic. After all, the prevailing thought is that "once an alcoholic, always an alcoholic."

That is not my professional opinion — nor has that been my professional or personal experience.

If your heart is open and you have a real desire to heal — and if you are willing to reach inside yourself and grab on tight to some genuine courage — then anything is possible.

My final words of support.

If you are struggling with a difficult life challenge, and you're engaging in addictive behaviors to cope, and you are questioning whether you can be an effective parent, <u>seek help now</u>.

Don't subject your children to the extreme stress that they inevitably experience when living with a parent who is an alcoholic / addict. Your children deserve better. And help is available.

There are circumstances, of course, where a parent is posing a danger to their children due to their addiction (driving drunk, flying into a blackout rage, etc.) Those situations are very sad, but they do happen. When that's the case, legal intervention is typically necessary, as well as registration at a live-in recovery facility, or other action steps to separate parent and child, at least temporarily.

In other situations, this kind of separation is not necessary. In some cases, even if you are immersed in your recovery, you can still be a good role model and source of unconditional love for your child.

Through your own recovery, you are modeling important life lessons for your child, like:

"Sometimes grown ups do unhealthy, self-destructive things. But if you are willing to learn to love yourself, be courageous, get help, and commit to doing better, then change is possible. Improvement is possible. Transformation is possible. Anything is possible."

Healthy love is the answer to every problem.

Everyone deserves love and everyone has the capacity to find deep reserves of self-love, again.

Where there is love, addictions cannot survive.

Where there is love, your children can thrive.

CLOSING WORDS

These three quotes sum up pretty much what I've expressed in this book — in a total of just 56 words:

"Kids are like a mirror, what they see and hear they do. Be a good reflection for them." — Kevin Heath
"Live so that when your children think of fairness and integrity, they think of you." — H. Jackson Brown, Jr.
"To bring up a child in the way he should go, travel that way yourself." — Josh Billings

Travel through this world with courage, fairness and integrity.

Be the best possible role model you can be.

Your child is looking to you to set the tone, to set the rules, to implement the consequences, to light the path, to lead the way. Don't let your child down. This is your responsibility — and it's a beautiful one.

Your child's wellbeing is anchored in you.

Know this. Claim this task with your whole heart. Do your job well.

It starts with you.

WORKSHEETS AND TOOLS

(Sample) Behavior Chart

Included in this section is a sample behavior chart for an eight-year-old. Tailor the chart to your child's age and choose consequences that are most likely to motivate cooperation. A blank chart, ready for you to use, follows after the sample,

If your child's schedule is different on the weekend from during the week, you may want to create a separate chart for weekends (and holidays).

You can also be creative with the chart, having your child place stickers or stars when he or she completes a task, and a sad emoticon (sad smiley face) when something has not been completed.

Older children (age 9 and above) often enjoy creating and filling in the chart themselves. In that case, let these children assume as much responsibility for their chart as possible.

If feasible, create a computerized version of the chart. This makes it easier to make changes, and print-out weekly and weekend charts.

Encourage your child to take pride in his or her chart. It is not intended to be seen as a harsh task master. To the contrary, it is a tool to support children in achieving their goals and enjoying their well-earned privileges.

You, as the parent, will need to keep your own tally of the number of consequences that your child has incurred in a given week. Keeping track of this on a calendar can work well (i.e., if your child incurs consequences in a given week, which result in forfeiting two playdates, simply cancel out the next two playdates that are scheduled on your calendar. If the playdates have not been scheduled yet, one option is to have a running list of consequences on your calendar, which carry over from week to week, and which can be assigned to relevant events, such as playdates that come up for scheduling.)

The point is to create a system that allows you to keep track of the consequences that have been incurred — whether that be with a calendar, or some other method.

Time	Action	M	T	W	Th	F	Sat	S	Consequence for breaking the rule
6:00 AM	Get up on time								No iPad for a day
6:05 AM	Brush teeth, wash face, get dressed								Cannot watch favorite TV program that evening
6:15 AM	Make my bed								No dessert for a day
6:20 AM	Breakfast								
6:25 AM	Put lunch in backpack								No money for snack at school
6:30 AM	Be ready to get in the car								Take the bus
7:30 PM -3:00 PM	At school: pay close attention & follow rules								No iPad for one day, no sleepover for one night
3:30 PM	Bring backpack into house from car								Extra chores
3:40 PM	Snack								

Time	Action	M	T	W	Th	F	Sat	S	Consequence for breaking the rule
3:45 PM	Homework								No TV or computer privileges for a day
5:00 PM	Chores								No playtime
5:30 PM	Play outside								
6:00 PM	Dinner								
6:45 PM	Bath, brush teeth								Miss next playdate
7:00 PM	Pack back pack for next day; put out school clothes								No iPad for one day
7:15 PM	Show parent this chart								Miss next playdate & sleepover
7:30 PM	TV / computer time								
8:00 PM	Bedtime								No electronics for one day
Always	Be polite, co-operate, not talk back or be sassy, etc.								Forfeit electronics, playdates, sleepovers. Do extra chores, etc.

Time	Activity	M	T	W	Th	F	Sat	S	Consequence for breaking the rule

(Sample) Parenting Plan Worksheet

Our parenting philosophy:

"We believe that our children need guidance and direction as to how to manage their abundant energy.

We don't believe in stifling their individuality and creativity, but we recognize that our children need our leadership and input as we equip them with skills to navigate life.

We believe that our primary responsibility is to teach our children right from wrong. To that end, we have reasonable rules in place, with consequences for non-compliance.

We are committed to applying consequences consistently, when necessary. Otherwise our children will not respect our authority or find us to be credible."

Basic rules and associated (age-appropriate) consequences.

- Rule: Be polite and cooperate.
  Consequence: Forfeit iPad privileges for one day.
- Rule: Do chores before going outside to play.
  Consequence: No playdate for one day.
- Rule: Keep your room tidy.
  Consequence: Miss your favorite TV program that night.
- Rule: Put your clothes in the hamper.
  Consequence: No cell phone for one day.
- Rule: No sitting with feet on the furniture.
  Consequence: Forfeit your favorite dessert.
- Rule: No teasing your little brother (or sister).
  Consequence: No going to the mall on the weekend.
- Rule: No watching TV or talking on the phone until homework & chores are done.
  Consequence: TV and phone privileges revoked for one day.
- Rule: No dessert or snack before a meal.
  Consequence: Forfeit your favorite dessert.

- Rule: No electronics / computer surfing until the designated computer time.
  Consequence: Forfeit computer time for one day.
- Rule: Show caregiver your behavior chart at the beginning of caregiver's shift.
  Consequence: Do additional chores.

Our phone numbers (in case the caregiver needs to reach us with a question or concern.)

[insert name] [insert telephone number]
[insert name] [insert telephone number]

Alternate contact (in case neither of us are unavailable.)

[insert name] [insert telephone number]

Conversation Script for Conducting a Successful "Family Meeting"

If you need to let your children know about some new rules and consequences that you are putting into place, this script can get that conversation rolling.

"_____ and _____, (insert children's names) I asked you to be here today because there's something I want to talk about.

It's very important that you listen all the way until the end. I'll let you know when it's time to for you to talk and share your thoughts.

Lately, I have not been pleased about _____ (identify the behavior or situation).

When _____ happens, it is not acceptable. As your parent, it is my responsibility to make things right.

From now on, in our home, there are some new rules — and new consequences for not following those rules.

I am setting these rules because they can help you grow up to be the best person you can be.

I am going to share them with you now."

[Read your entire plan out loud, explaining all of the new rules and consequences. Explain that at the end of each day you and your child will meet to review the chart.]

- For younger children (ages 4 to 7), you will initiate the nightly meeting.
- Older children (ages 8 and up) need to bring their chart to you each night. Emphasize that they need to initiate this "chart review" session. If they don't, a consequence will follow.

These new rules will create a much happier home for everyone. I plan to insert them into a chart and put the chart _____ (explain where the chart will be located. Example: on the bulletin board or the refrigerator) so you can see these rules every day.

Thank you for listening. Do you have any questions?"

(For even more tips on how to hold a successful "family meeting," above and beyond what you learned in this book, check out this digital book called: *The Life Guide On How To Get Your Kids To Cooperate — And Help Them Become the BEST Grown-Ups They Can Be.* http://drsuzannegelb.com/get-kids-cooperate/).

Fifty Things to Talk About at Dinner[1]

1. What was the best part of your day?
2. What are you grateful for today?
3. Does anyone have a good joke to tell?
4. How did your test go at school?
5. Did you help anyone today?
6. What is something really nice that someone did for you today?
7. If a friend was being bullied, what would you do?
8. What's your favorite movie? Why?
9. What's your favorite book? Why?
10. If you could invite someone to dinner, who would that be? What would you talk about?
11. If you had one wish that was guaranteed to come true, what would you wish for?
12. If you could be someone famous for a day, who would you be?
13. If you could travel anywhere in the world, where would you go?
14. If you could live anywhere in the world, where would you live?
15. What's the nicest thing about yourself, and why?
16. If you could travel back in time, what era would you like to visit?
17. What's something really nice that a friend has done for you recently?
18. What are you most proud of?
19. If there was one thing you could change in the world, what would that be?
20. If there was one thing you could change about yourself, what would that be?
21. If you could change one thing about your parents, what would that be?

---

[1] This list can be found at DrSuzanneGelb.com bit.ly/20jWE9e.

22. If you could change one thing about your school, what would that be?
23. Who is your favorite teacher, and why?
24. What do you think about home schooling?
25. How do you feel when someone is mad at you?
26. Who is your closest friend at school? What do you like most about them?
27. Do you know why people get divorced? Are any of your friends' parents divorced?
28. Do you like your name? If you could pick a different name, what would you pick?
29. If you could make dinner for us tomorrow night, what would you prepare?
30. If you could decorate your room however you wanted, how would it look?
31. What fun activity would you like us to do as a family?
32. What is your favorite room or area of our home?
33. What do you like most about our family?
34. What are two goals that you have for this year?
35. What would you do if you found out that your best friend was lying to her parents?
36. Who is your favorite movie star or singer? Why?
37. Who is your favorite teacher or coach? Why?
38. What is your favorite activity that you like to do with your friends?
39. What is one of the most important lessons that you have learned?
40. What did you do during recess today?
41. How did your [insert after school activity] go today?
42. Describe yourself in three words. Then describe me in three words. (You can go around the table and have everyone take turns describing each other.)
43. If you were President of the United States, what is the first law that you would pass?
44. What is your favorite vacation memory?
45. How do you like this dinner? What else do you think might make it better?

46. If you could change one thing about your day today, what would it be?
47. Put a glass on the table that's half filled with water. Ask your children: Is the glass half full or half empty?
48. If you were an architect, what kind of building would you design?
49. Out of all the people in our family, who are you most similar to?
50. Tell your children (age-appropriate): "I need to make a decision about something at work. [Briefly share the situation.] Can you help me?" Children love to feel that their opinion matters... and often, their ideas are quite creative and surprising!

Family Calendars to Track Appointments, Assignments, After-School Activities, Etc.

Google Calendar
   Free and part of your Google account.
   https://bit.ly/2TONQ1y

Family Time Planner
   Flexible and colorful tool. Fee-based. Syncs with Microsoft Outlook. No advertisements.
   https://bit.ly/2ueCrZQ

Cozi
   A free app and website where you can manage activities, appointments, shopping lists, meal plans and to do lists all in one place, for everyone in the family to access.
   https://bit.ly/1et7d1b

RESOURCES

Articles to Read

(Written by Dr. Gelb, Published Online)

Psychology Today

Three Lessons You Must Teach Your Kids. (The sooner the better. But it's never too late.)
   bit.ly/1QndzkF

Why "Bribing" Your Child With Treats... Doesn't Work. And What Does.
   bit.ly/1UsyRm4

Raising Kids Who Love Reading and Devour Books Voraciously.
   https://bit.ly/2Ctb42R

The Huffington Post

"Mommy, do you love your blog more than me?" What to do if your child feels in competition with your work.
   https://bit.ly/2CuCFk3

3 Ways to Stop Your Teen From Making Risky Choices.
   bit.ly/Gelb_Teens_HuffPO

Maria Shriver

Good Parenting Isn't Complicated — Here's Why.
   bit.ly/1QlQQsE

Mind Body Green

7 Dangerous Lessons We Need To Stop Teaching Our Kids.
   bit.ly/Dangerous-Lessons

6 Self-Sabotaging Habits You Need To Drop Right Now
   https://bit.ly/2WdNo9R

Family Advocate, American Bar Association

Time-Out. Getting the Most Out of This Popular Discipline Tactic.
   https://bit.ly/2FdxXYy

Raising an Organized Child In a Blended Family.
   https://bit.ly/2HJgxFW

When the Other Parent Doesn't Play Fair.
   bit.ly/1QmYYpq

ABOUT THE AUTHOR

Dr. Suzanne Gelb, Ph.D., J.D. is a psychologist, life coach, TV commentator and author.

Dr. Gelb's inspiring insights on personal growth have been featured on more than 200 radio programs, 260 TV interviews, and online on TIME, Newsweek, Forbes, The Huffington Post, NBC's Today, Positively Positive, The Muse and many other places. She served as a parenting expert writer for *Hawaii Parent* magazine for over 14 years and appeared regularly on television to share tips on a parenting segment for 6 years.

As a contributing writer to *Psychology Today*, on her regular column, "All Grown Up," Dr. Gelb's articles on parenting include, **10 Vital Life Lessons to Teach Your Kids Before They Turn 10**, and **10 Ways to Become the Parent Your Children Really Need**. Her powerful article, **7 Dangerous Lessons We Need To Stop Teaching Our Kids,** was published on Mind Body Green.

Dr. Gelb believes that it is never too late to become the person — and parent — you want to be. Strong. Confident. Calm. Creative. Free of the burdens that have held you back — no matter what has happened in the past.

To learn more, visit DrSuzanneGelb.com.

PRAISE FOR... IT STARTS WITH YOU

From Parents

"I always thought it was my kids' fault for not cooperating. After reading this book, I realized that if I wanted them to cooperate, I needed to change how I was parenting. That's exactly what happened (I made some changes, and then they did too). So remarkably simple... so incredibly effective. Wow!"
— Belinda K

"I've read a lot of parenting books, but this one is totally unique. Dr. Gelb has captured the essence of effective parenting in this gem of a book and taken the mystery (and the struggle) out of raising, happy, fun-loving, well-adjusted children. Beautifully written, practical, easy-to-read. Finally, peace at home ... thanks to this book!"
— Mark B

"The stories that Dr. Gelb shares at the beginning of the chapters in the book about the parents she's worked with — and their successes — are so inspiring to a parent like me who is pulling her hair out, trying to get my kids to listen. The self-reflection exercises in the book are game-changers. I went from feeling frustrated and helpless, to empowered and pleased with the changes I see in my kids (and my whole family) as I implement the tools and solutions in this book."
— Tracy L

"This book is so readable and was a major turning point in my understanding of parenting — reading it saved my family."
— Bob T

From Children

"Mommy read this book and now we have all our rules on a chart on the fridge. I know what I am supposed to do and I don't forget things. Also, we don't yell as much. It's awesome!"
— Ryan, 8

"Daddy doesn't get mad and yell at everyone, and slam doors like he used to. Mommy says it's because he read this parenting book. I am so happy, thank you."
— Adam, 9

"My parents never used to listen to anything I had to say. It was always, "Because I said so." I used to cry myself to sleep, and not want to get up in the mornings. Lately [after they read this book] they've been really listening to me when I have something to say. For the first time ever, I feel heard in my family, and like I belong, and that I want to be part of this family. It's so different at home now... so much better."
— Jenny, 12

"I used to get mad and kick the furniture when Daddy and Mommy told me to do stuff that they didn't do — like "Make your bed," but they never made theirs. Then Grandma gave them this book. Now they make their beds. too. That's more fair. I'm not mad anymore."
— Laurie, 10

"My dad read this book and now he comes home for dinner and he talks to me about my day. He used to stay late at work, past my bedtime. I'm so happy to see my dad at dinner, and so is my mom."
— Jimmy, 11

"When I grow up, I want to be just like Mommy. She says this book is helping her do her best."
— Katie, 7

INDEX

A
acting out, 105, 114, 132, 135
addiction, 5, 149-50, 152-53, 155
afraid, 14, 36, 43, 50, 104, 107
age-appropriate, 12, 14-17, 27, 48, 64, 84, 99, 101, 109, 151-52, 161-62, 168
alcoholism, 149, 151, 155
angrily, 17, 23, 71, 98, 101
angry, 23, 65, 69, 85, 100-01, 109, 116, 128, 130, 152
articles to read, 170
attention, 16, 56-57, 78, 82, 86, 95, 106-09, 112, 114, 122, 124, 137, 141, 144-46, 159

B
babysitter, 3, 22, 25, 56-57, 132-33, 136
behavior, 6, 8-11, 13, 15-17, 19-28, 32-34, 40, 44, 48-49, 51, 53-61, 63, 65-66, 68, 70-73, 77, 79, 87, 94, 97, 99, 100-01, 104-06, 110, 115, 119, 123, 125-26, 130, 132, 134-37, 141, 143-46, 149-54, 158, 163-64, 173
blow up, 100, 119-21
bullied, 83-84, 87, 166

C
cell phone, 21, 26, 59, 77-79, 81, 99, 108, 123, 132, 139-40, 162
charts, 6, 9-10, 18, 23, 25, 50-51, 67, 101, 158
childcare conflicts, 133
chores, 5, 18-19, 26, 40, 49, 51, 65, 98, 105, 120, 129, 159-60, 162-63
clear policies, 139
communication, 34, 62, 88, 97, 100, 106, 108-110, 123-24, 129, 135
confidence, 37, 40, 131, 145, 171
coping, 104, 111, 151
conversation script, 6, 164
cooperate, 1, 5, 9, 11, 27, 47, 49, 120, 162, 165, 178
consequence, 10, 15-27, 49, 51, 56, 72, 75-76, 97, 99, 105, 123, 139, 159-164
consequences, 5-6, 9-21, 25-27, 34, 40, 48, 51, 55, 57-59, 73-77, 79, 94, 97-99, 101, 108, 115, 123, 129, 136, 157-59, 162, 164
consistency, 25, 28, 93-94, 113, 115, 134-35, 137
consistent, 3, 5, 22, 25, 34, 51, 58, 93-95, 99, 110, 113, 121, 129
consistently, 6, 10, 12, 16, 25, 27, 56, 76, 86, 93, 105-6, 123, 137, 162

D

dating, 70-77, 78-80
defiant, 10, 32, 54-55
de-stressing, 115, 121
discipline, 12, 131, 133-34, 144
dishonest, 29-30
disorganized, 36, 47-48
disrespectful, 57, 97, 105
divorce, 89, 91, 95, 100, 111-18, 167, 171, 173
Dr. Maya Angelou, 6

E

emotional eating, 66, 173
emotional management, 66
emotion, 112, 122, 127-28, 143
emotions, 66-67, 73, 85, 90-91, 93, 95, 99-100, 109, 113-14, 116-17, 119-21, 124, 126-28, 131, 135, 143, 153-54
excellence, 3, 40, 135
explode, 11, 99-100, 119, 121
explosive, 100, 120-21, 124, 152

F

fair, 5, 16, 18-19, 24, 47, 98, 144-45
family meeting, 17, 57-58, 73-74, 164-65
favoring, 142-43
favoritism, 142-43, 145, 148
fear, 15, 43-44, 50, 62, 90, 107, 122, 124, 128, 150, 153
fearfully, 101
feelings, 31-32, 44, 51, 61-62, 64, 69, 73, 90-92, 95, 100-1, 103-4, 109-10, 113, 115, 118, 120, 122, 127-28, 130-1, 143, 145, 152-54

fifteen second rule, 127
fight, 34, 104, 106, 111
forgive, 128, 130-31, 143, 154
forgiving, 128, 130
friends, 26, 29, 40-41, 54, 60-63, 68, 75, 77-78, 80, 85, 89-90, 92-94, 111, 130, 151, 167
frustrated, 36-37, 53, 91, 116, 122, 126, 135

G

good habits, 66-67
grandparent, 3, 25, 56, 61, 104, 132-33, 136, 139-40
greedy, 10
Google, 80-81, 169
grades, 21, 36, 40, 85, 130, 151
guilt, 43-44, 95, 100-01, 117, 122
guilty, 11, 43-44, 95, 101-02, 112, 148

H

happiness, 28, 42, 95. 112
happier, 27, 94, 101-02, 109, 115, 137, 164
harmony, 3, 139
healing, 32, 43, 45, 92. 107
homework, 20-21, 24, 34, 36-38, 46, 49-51, 81, 98, 105, 130, 160, 162, 173
hostility, 32, 98

I

inconsiderate, 53-54
inconsistent, 9, 14, 38, 72
inner child, 32, 43, 45, 107-08

L

learned behaviors, 10
lenient, 10, 14, 30-32, 54, 72, 95, 126, 129
listen, 1-2, 9, 33, 40, 67, 84, 86, 88, 91-92, 104, 106, 108, 112-13, 115-16, 164
listening, 24, 27, 34, 62, 81, 106, 108, 121, 165
love, 5, 7, 13, 23, 27, 32, 39, 43, 52, 69, 73, 82, 85, 93-96, 108, 110, 112-15, 117-19, 122, 124, 132, 139, 141-43, 145-48, 152, 155, 168, 170-71, 175
low self-esteem, 36-37, 39, 41, 50, 61, 145

M

manipulative, 10, 29-30, 34, 105
manners, 53
messy, 16, 46-48
misbehave, 22, 23, 119
misbehavior, 11, 13, 15, 21-22, 34, 101, 115
miscommunication, 135
mistake, 37-38, 41, 43-44, 104, 107, 138, 146, 173

N

nagging, 25, 46, 52, 97
nanny, 104
non-compliance, 5, 14, 17, 20, 51, 58, 162

O

online activity, 75, 80
organizational issues, 50
organizational skills, 40, 48, 51

overachieving, 41-42, 44
overeat, 66, 171
overeating, 64-65, 67-68, 152-53, 173
overprotective, 14, 37-38
overreact, 84, 88, 141
overweight, 5, 64-65, 87

P

parental consequences, 40
parenting plan, 33, 136, 162
parenting style, 27, 30, 38, 55, 97, 125, 138, 144
patient, 15-17, 30, 33, 94
peace of mind, 8, 28
pent-up emotions, 69, 116-17
perfection, 40, 136, 151
perfectionist, 41
perfectionistic, 45, 50, 55
phone, 23, 27, 33, 58, 60-61, 75, 78-80, 93, 124, 136, 139, 147, 162-63
positive discipline, 12
praise, 26, 38, 40, 68, 141, 146, 173
privilege, 19-22, 58, 76, 99, 123
privileges, 19-21, 26, 31, 58-59, 77, 99, 112, 123, 139, 158, 160, 162
procrastination, 46-47
problem solver, 88
promises, 128-30
punish, 99, 105, 125
punishing, 11-12, 16, 44

R

reminding, 8, 24, 46
respect, 2-3, 15, 27, 34, 38, 43, 47, 56, 58, 71, 81, 162
respectful, 28, 57, 100, 105
resources, 6, 170
rewards, 26, 172
role model, 2-3, 6, 8-10, 47-49, 54-55, 57, 62, 71-72, 81, 94-95, 97, 105, 107-08, 112, 120, 129-30, 134, 138, 152, 155, 157, 170
routines, 93-94, 113, 115
rude, 10, 53-56, 96-97, 100
rudeness, 53-54, 98-99
rules, 2, 4, 6, 9-15, 17-18, 21-25, 27, 30-32, 34, 47-49, 51, 56-57, 59, 66, 72-76, 79, 81, 93-95, 97-98, 100-02, 113, 115, 123, 129, 133-37, 139, 157, 159, 162, 164

S

school, 19, 21, 26, 36-37, 40-41, 46-47, 50-53, 57, 60-61, 68, 70, 78-79, 83-84, 86-92, 94, 103-04, 123, 137, 141, 145, 151, 159-60, 166-67, 169, 171-72
script, 6, 49, 57, 148, 164
selfish, 10
self-care, 93, 116, 118, 121-22
self-confidence, 38-39, 51-52
self-esteem, 36-39, 41, 43, 50-51, 61, 67, 142, 145, 147, 150, 171-73
self-respect, 6, 70-72, 76
sex, 70-73, 77, 79-80, 171
shy, 60-63, 108, 171, 173
siblings, 12, 60, 142-43, 148
silent treatment, 105
sleepover, 19, 97-99, 159-60
sleepovers, 26, 58
spouse, 2-3, 30, 32, 37, 56, 72, 104, 106, 120, 129, 136, 138, 142
stepparent, 129, 132-33, 136, 138
stress, 2, 67, 90, 93-94, 117, 120-22, 151-52, 154, 172-73
stress management, 116-17, 120-21
stressful, 66, 83-84, 90, 104, 114, 116-17
stressed, 2, 41, 69, 90-91, 118, 120-21
strict, 14, 30-32, 55, 125
structure, 30, 51, 89, 91, 102
succeeding, 34, 41-42
successful, 1, 13, 40, 74, 81, 94, 141, 164-65
supervise, 40, 55-57, 74-75, 77, 80, 86
supervision, 9, 74-76, 79, 129

T

tantrum, 16-17, 27, 55, 119, 122
tantrums, 11, 32, 119, 122, 124
teachable moment, 129, 137-38
teachable moments, 129
teased, 83-84
tech-addicted, 78-79
technology, 79-81
the best, 27-28, 31, 33-34, 38, 42-45, 66, 69, 74, 86, 94-96, 114, 138, 145-46, 152-53, 157, 164, 166
temper, 119
time-management, 50
time-out, 19, 33, 172
tools, 13, 31, 75, 80, 123, 147, 153, 158

U

underachiever, 36-37, 41-42
uncooperative, 119-20, 123
unfair, 9, 32, 36, 52, 55, 99, 108, 142, 145, 147, 153
unified front, 10, 30, 33, 126

V

video clips to watch, 172
video games, 20, 26, 29, 34, 49, 67, 134
visual charts, 9, 50

W

withdrawing, 19, 104
withdrawn, 62, 87, 103-06, 108, 110
worksheets, 158
worry, 60, 70, 87, 95, 103, 120, 132
wrong, 12, 36, 38, 84, 104, 145, 152, 162

www.ingramcontent.com/pod-product-compliance
Lightning Source LLC
Chambersburg PA
CBHW030053100526
44591CB00008B/128